I0047837

Growth prospects have dimmed amid rising financial risks

- The path of global economic recovery remains uneven and highly uncertain as the world continues to deal with compounded shocks from the scars left by the COVID-19 pandemic, the wide-ranging impacts of the Russian invasion of Ukraine, and the resulting surge in inflation. The consequences of attempts by monetary authorities—particularly in the United States (US) and Europe—to respond to these shocks have also revealed unforeseen sources of financial risk. Despite the rapid rise in interest rates, inflation in many economies is higher than historical averages amid slowing growth, high indebtedness, and rising concerns over financial stability. Consequently, the International Monetary Fund forecasts slower growth of 3.0% in 2023 and 2024, with advanced economies accounting for much of the slowdown. Downside risks dominate the outlook. Stubborn inflation means authorities will have to maintain a bias toward tighter monetary policy. A risk-off shock to distressed financial institutions could roil markets and adversely affect credit conditions and public finances. Monetary policy will have to balance the need to control inflation with financial stability considerations, complemented by fiscal consolidation.

- The recovery of the People's Republic of China (PRC) will support developing Asia's projected growth of 4.8% in 2023 and 4.7% in 2024. The economic reopening of the PRC has improved growth prospects for the region via greater demand for goods and services and supply chain linkages. Many economies in the region have reopened to tourists, and the end of travel restrictions in the PRC will further lift the outlook for tourism. Downside risks remain, however. Financial stability issues in advanced economies could have global spillover effects. Persistent inflation exerts pressure for continued monetary tightening, the effects of which are starting to be felt in some countries. Commodity prices also remain vulnerable to surges should there be a further escalation in the Russian invasion of Ukraine.

- GDP growth in the Pacific is projected at 3.3% in 2023 and 2.8% in 2024, sustaining the subregion's rebound from COVID-19. In Papua New Guinea, increased output outside the resource sector will underpin economic growth in 2023 and 2024. Tourism will continue to drive growth in Fiji albeit at a more modest pace with increasing competition from other tourist destinations. Other tourism-driven economies such as the Cook Islands and Samoa are also benefiting from the lifting of travel restrictions along with increased public investment spending. The outlook for the subregion is weighed by downside risks. In the short term, inflation remains persistent albeit declining, and many economies are sensitive to international commodity price shocks. There is uncertainty as to the pace of the resumption of stalled projects and an expected uneven recovery in tourism exacerbated by possible economic scarring from the pandemic. Vulnerability to disasters is a long-standing structural risk as demonstrated in March 2023 by devastating cyclones and earthquakes in Vanuatu.

- The US economy grew by 1.3% in the first quarter (Q1) of 2023, slower than the previous quarter but stronger than initially expected. The deceleration was driven by an 11.5% decline in investment due to normalization in inventory levels. This was offset by a rebound in private consumption and public spending. Interest rate hikes are likely to weigh on the economy in 2023 and 2024, further weakening investment and slowing consumption

GDP Growth (%, annual)

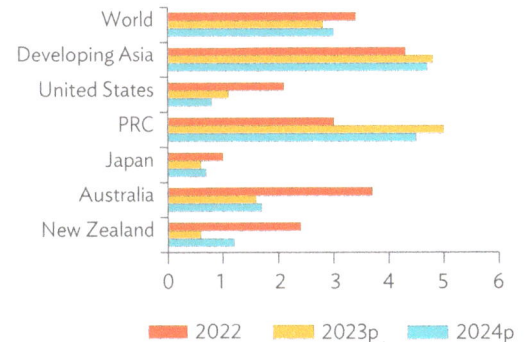

ADB = Asian Development Bank, GDP = gross domestic product, p = projection, PRC = People's Republic of China.

Notes: Developing Asia as defined by ADB. Figures are based on ADB estimates except for world, Australia, and New Zealand GDP growth.

Sources: ADB. Asian Development Outlook Database (accessed 4 July 2023); Consensus Economics. 2023. *Asia Pacific Consensus Forecasts May 2023*. London; International Monetary Fund. 2023. *World Economic Outlook Update, July 2023: Near-Term Resilience, Persistent Challenges*. Washington, DC.

GDP Growth in Developing Asia (%, annual)

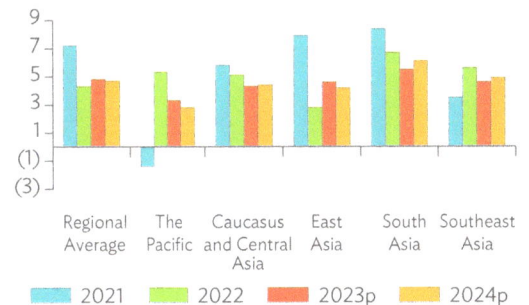

GDP = gross domestic product, p = projection.

Source: ADB. Asian Development Outlook Database (accessed 4 July 2023).

Average Spot Price of Brent Crude Oil
(monthly, $/barrel)

Source: World Bank. 2023. *World Bank Commodity Price Data (Pink Sheet)* (accessed 18 June 2023).

Food Prices
(January 2021 = 100)

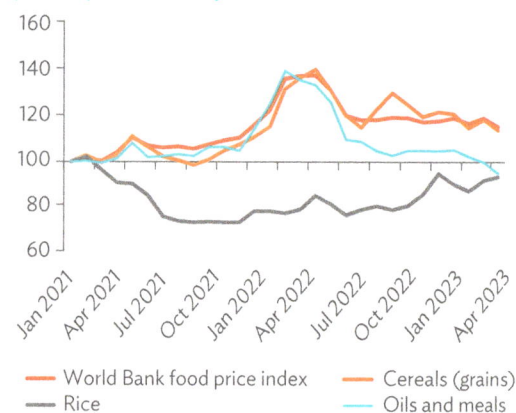

Legend: World Bank food price index, Cereals (grains), Rice, Oils and meals

Sources: ADB calculations using data from World Bank. 2023. *World Bank Commodity Price Data (Pink Sheet)* (accessed 18 June 2023).

growth. Persistent inflation and a surprisingly resilient labor market will continue to exert pressure on the US Federal Reserve toward a tightening bias notwithstanding the pause in June. US GDP growth forecasts have been revised upward to 1.1% in 2023 and down to 0.8% in 2024, largely on account of the robust Q1 performance though the momentum is expected to slow for the rest of 2023 and into 2024.

- After slowing in Q4 2022, year-on-year GDP growth in the PRC accelerated to 4.5% during Q1 2023 and further to 6.3% in Q2 2023. Following the easing of public health measures in December 2022, growth picked up in contact-intensive services and retail sales, but industrial activity and merchandise exports lagged. Travel restrictions were removed early in 2023—though outbound international trips remain limited—helping to sustain a strong recovery in domestic tourism which would help offset slowing exports. GDP is expected to grow by 5.0% in 2023 and 4.5% in 2024 as government policies remain accommodative. Measures to boost the housing market appear to be supporting the price of new homes in leading urban areas, and fiscal authorities have committed to providing more stimulus to spur growth in the broader economy. In contrast with other major economies, a reduction in benchmark lending rates by the People's Bank of China in June signals further easing in monetary conditions in the short term.

- The Japanese economy expanded at an annualized pace of 2.7% in Q1 2023, driven by a recovery in inbound tourism and service consumption. Foreign tourists from most source markets—excluding the PRC and Taipei,China—reached pre-pandemic levels as of April 2023. The recovery in tourism is expected to be sustained with the continued expansion of airline capacities and increased international travel from the PRC. Economic activity was supported by domestic demand with resilient private consumption and growth in capital spending driven by a rise in inventories. The government's decision in May to handle COVID-19 in a similar way to seasonal influenza is also expected to boost consumer confidence and sustain growth in service consumption. GDP growth is projected at 0.6% in 2023 and 0.7% in 2024.

- Australian economic growth decelerated in Q1 2023 amid a high inflationary environment. Seasonally adjusted GDP posted a weak 0.2% expansion as household and government expenditure softened and imports grew faster than exports. On the production side, manufacturing grew by 2.4% as food production recovered from weather-induced delays in the previous quarter, while metal production rose driven by higher global demand. Notable advances in the services sector were observed in wholesale trade, media and telecommunications, and health care. Agriculture contracted due to the disruption of cotton planting in New South Wales while mining contracted due to planned maintenance and shutdowns and weather events. Although goods inflation moderated, price pressures remained a concern as the compensation of employees rose 2.4% in Q1 2023. A tight labor market due to shortages of skilled labor has pushed labor costs, prompting the Reserve Bank of Australia to raise its cash rate target to manage inflation. Full-year growth is expected to be at 1.6% in 2023 and 1.7% in 2024.

- The New Zealand economy entered recession as activity fell by 0.1% in Q1 2023 following a 0.7% drop in Q4 2022. Service industries reported the largest drop of 0.6%, driven by weaker business services such as advertising, market research and management services, and transport support services. Manufacturing was down by 1.1% due to lower output in petroleum, chemical, polymer, and rubber product manufacturing as well as lower production of wood and paper products. Agriculture recorded a second consecutive quarter

Prices of Export Commodities
(January 2021 = 100)

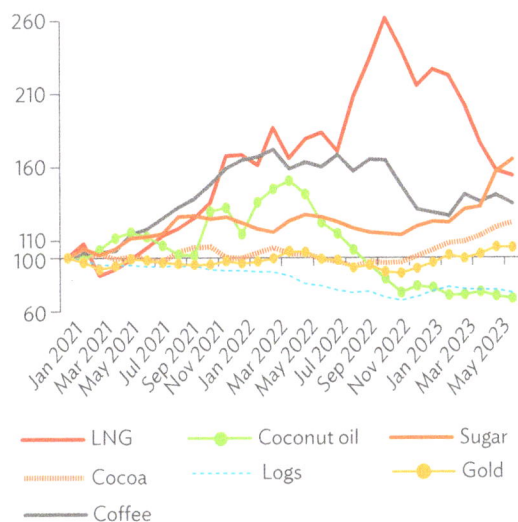

LNG = liquefied natural gas.

Sources: ADB calculations using data from World Bank.
2023. *World Bank Commodity Price Data (Pink Sheet)*
(accessed 18 June 2023).

decline of 0.7%. On the expenditure side, the primary drag on GDP was the drop in distribution inventories for retail and wholesale businesses, resulting in a 3.0% decline in gross capital formation. Tropical cyclones Hale and Gabrielle in late-January and mid-February 2023 and the resulting flooding created significant damage and disruption to horticulture, transport support services, and education services. Exports were also down 2.5% mainly due to the fall in travel services. Although the economy is forecast to grow by 0.6% in 2023 and 1.2% in 2024, the Reserve Bank of New Zealand's aggressive hiking of interest rates to arrest inflation may lead to further contractions up to 2024 according to analysts. The unemployment rate could also rise, with migration-led labor supply expansion amid weaker demand.

Mixed outcome for commodity prices amid uncertainties

- The Brent crude oil price declined by 7.8% in Q1 2023 compared to Q4 2022. This is the third consecutive quarter price drop. Prices were initially expected to rise following the PRC's reopening and recovery of air travel, but it has been tempered by tighter monetary policy in advanced economies and weaker global growth. Nonetheless, the Brent crude oil price is expected to stabilize in 2023 and slightly increase in 2024 due to the recovery of global demand and production cuts by the Organization of Petroleum Exporting Countries and 10 affiliated countries.

- The World Bank food price index barely changed in Q1 2023 amid mixed outcomes for different commodities. Grain prices were 4.6% lower in Q1 2023 compared to Q4 2022 as wheat and corn prices fell. The Black Sea Grain Initiative—which facilitated the movement of Ukraine's agricultural products to the global market—has helped ease price pressures relating to the difficulties in shipping grain. The expiration of several export bans and improving global supply chain conditions have also contributed to the price decline. The price indexes for most other food commodities—notably sugar and fruit—rose in Q1 but meat prices remained stable. The food price index is expected to decline by 7.8% in 2023 and by 2.8% in 2024. Removal of trade restrictions and lower global growth would push prices lower. However, the escalation of the geopolitical situation and extreme weather events could have an opposite impact.

- Prices of natural gas plunged amid higher global supply. Despite the loss of Russian exports, global production of natural gas remained stable as other suppliers filled the gap. In particular, the Japanese liquefied natural gas import price dropped 11% in Q1 2023 compared to Q4 2022. Aside from increased production, lower demand, higher inventories, and improved access to supplies are expected to push down liquefied natural gas prices by 2.3% in 2023 and 11.1% in 2024. A stronger-than-expected recovery of the PRC industrial sector or further decline of Russian natural gas exports could lead to higher prices, while further expansion of US natural gas production and a shift to coal by European countries could lead to further price declines.

- Prices for most other Pacific export commodities were higher in Q1 2023. Gold prices advanced by 9.2%, as investors sought safe-haven assets amid high inflation and continued geopolitical uncertainty. While gold prices are expected to gain 5.5% in 2023, they are projected to drop 7.9% in 2024 as the global economy recovers and inflation moderates. Price increases were also observed in the same period for cocoa (10.9%), sugar (8.5%), and logs (6.7%). Coffee prices remained relatively stable though coconut oil prices declined by 4.6% in Q1 2023. The full year forecast for 2023 is for higher prices for cocoa and sugar while log prices are expected to stabilize. Both coffee and coconut oil prices are forecast to post double-digit drops in 2023.

Tourist Departures Bound for Pacific Destinations
('000 persons, January to April totals)

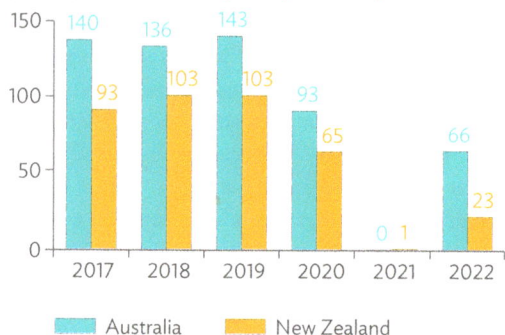

Sources: Government of Australia, Bureau of Statistics. Overseas Arrivals and Departures (accessed 14 June 2023), and Government of New Zealand, Stats NZ Tatauranga Aotearoa: International Travel and Migration (accessed 14 June 2023).

Outbound Tourism from Major Source Markets
(relative to pre–COVID-19 pandemic levels, monthly)

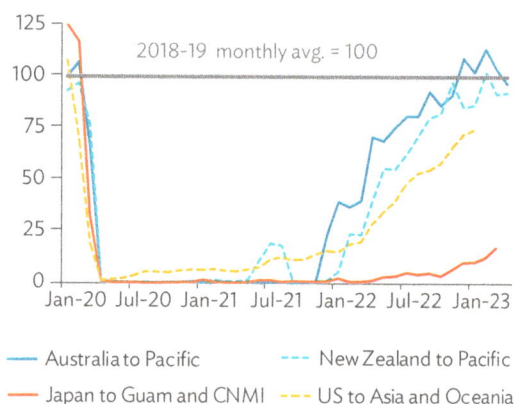

avg. = average, COVID-19 = coronavirus disease, CNMI = Commonwealth of the Northern Mariana Islands, US = United States.

Sources: Government of Australia, Bureau of Statistics. Overseas Arrivals and Departures (accessed 14 June 2023), Japan Tourism Marketing Co. Japanese Outbound Tourists Statistics (accessed 15 June 2023), Government of New Zealand, Stats NZ Tatauranga Aotearoa: International Travel and Migration (accessed 14 June 2023), and Government of the US, Department of Commerce International Trade Administration: US Outbound Travel to World Regions (accessed 15 June 2023).

Lead authors: Remrick Patagan, Noel Del Castillo, and Rommel Rabanal

Tourism recovery holds up in the South Pacific, remains stalled in the North

- The recovery in tourism arrivals to destinations in the South Pacific—buoyed by strong outbound travel from the main source markets of Australia and New Zealand—continued in early 2023. The resumption of outbound travel from key Asian markets continued to proceed at a conservative pace, slowing tourism prospects in the North Pacific.

- During the first 4 months of 2023, Australian tourism to major South Pacific destinations surpassed pre-pandemic levels. This was driven by sustained strong tourism in the largest destination, Fiji, where the number of Australian tourists during January–April 2023 reached 116% of the 2018–2019 average for the same months. Australian tourism to Samoa also recovered to usual levels (99%), but those to the Cook Islands (40%), Tonga (55%), and Vanuatu (68%) lagged to varying degrees, in part reflecting some lingering issues in the availability of flights and/or accommodations.

- The number of tourists from New Zealand visiting the South Pacific nearly recovered to pre-pandemic levels (92%). Tourism to Fiji had arrivals from New Zealand during the first 4 months of 2023 reaching 104% of the average for the same months in 2018–2019. The rebound in tourism from New Zealand to the South Pacific was broader based, with the Cook Islands, Samoa, and Tonga receiving more than 80% of their respective pre-pandemic tourist numbers. Recovery in the number of tourists from New Zealand was relatively weakest in Vanuatu at less than two-thirds of the usual numbers.

- In the North Pacific, tourism to Palau remains weak, largely owing to a delayed recovery in the resumption of outbound travel from its main markets in East Asia, particularly Japan. Proxying by the latest available data on outbound tourism from Japan to Palau's neighbors—Guam and the Commonwealth of the Northern Mariana Islands—Japanese tourism to the North Pacific continued to languish at only 10%–17% of pre-pandemic arrivals during Q1 2023.

References

Government of Australia, Bureau of Statistics. 2023. Australian National Accounts: National Income, Expenditure and Product. Media release. 7 June.

Consensus Economics. 2023. *Asia Pacific Consensus Forecasts May 2023.* London.

International Monetary Fund. 2023. *World Economic Outlook Update, July 2023: Near-Term Resilience, Persistent Challenges.* Washington, DC (April).

Government of New Zealand, Stats NZ Tatauranga Aotearoa. 2022. Gross domestic product: March 2023 quarter. Media release. 15 June.

World Bank. 2023. *Commodity Markets Outlook: Lower Prices, Little Relief, April 2023.* Washington, DC.

A. Zaki. 2023. New Zealand in recession as GDP falls for second quarter. *Radio New Zealand.* 15 June.

Strategizing for a sustainable economic recovery in the Cook Islands

Lead author: Lily-Anne Homasi

This article discusses the measures the Cook Islands has adopted to address heightened fiscal risks and support a sustainable post-pandemic recovery with potential lessons for neighboring countries.

Among ADB Pacific developing member countries (DMCs), the Cook Islands was the hardest hit by the coronavirus disease (COVID-19) pandemic with gross domestic product (GDP) contracting by 15.7% in fiscal year (FY) 2020 (ended 30 June) and 25.5% in FY2021. This was in large part due to the country's dependence on tourism, which—together with related activities—accounts for more than 60% of GDP. The economy has bounced back since the reopening of borders in January 2022. From July 2022 to May 2023, tourist arrivals numbered 114,089, exceeding the total number of visitors in FY2022 but this is still 33.6% below pre-pandemic levels.[1]

Recovering economic opportunities lost during the pandemic requires targeted and concerted efforts by government and national stakeholders to facilitate a strong and inclusive economic recovery. The government has pursued several reforms including developing and implementing the Cook Islands Economic Recovery Roadmap, instituting a cash management committee to strengthen the oversight and reporting on government finances and debt management, and pursuing a Public Service review to create a more cohesive and agile workforce. With continued strong support, these targeted reforms could mitigate future shocks and boost fiscal buffers which are critical for a smoother pathway to recovery.[2]

LASTING ECONOMIC IMPACTS OF THE COVID-19 PANDEMIC

COVID-19-induced contractions in the Cook Islands were concentrated in the private sector. Of the 37.2% decline in GDP in FY2021 relative to FY2019 levels (Figure 1), the services sector contributed 23.4 percentage points and industry 4.3 percentage points, with the tourism and construction sectors as the major drivers. The public sector saw large increases in recurrent government expenditure to mitigate the impacts of COVID-19, while public capital spending and public employment remained relatively constant.

However, this came at a cost. Before the pandemic, fiscal surpluses in the Cook Islands averaged 5.7% of GDP for the period FY2017–FY2019. This was supported by gains from successful tax reforms introduced in 2013 leading to an increase in total revenue from the equivalent of 36.4% of GDP in FY2016 to 40.2% in FY2019. The successive years of fiscal surplus since FY2016 have enabled the creation of a stabilization account which reached the equivalent of 11.4% of GDP by the end of FY2019. Debt financing—which has

been low and stable—fell from a peak of 26.4% of GDP in FY2016 to 15.9% of GDP in FY2020. Financing the economic response plan to moderate the impacts of the pandemic—alongside substantial declines in tax collections—created fiscal deficits averaging 14.4% of GDP between FY2020 and FY2022 (Figure 2). Government borrowing to finance the deficits increased the debt-to-GDP ratio to 46.2% over the same period.

Figure 1: Tourism-Dependent Pacific Economies GDP Relative to Pre-Pandemic Levels

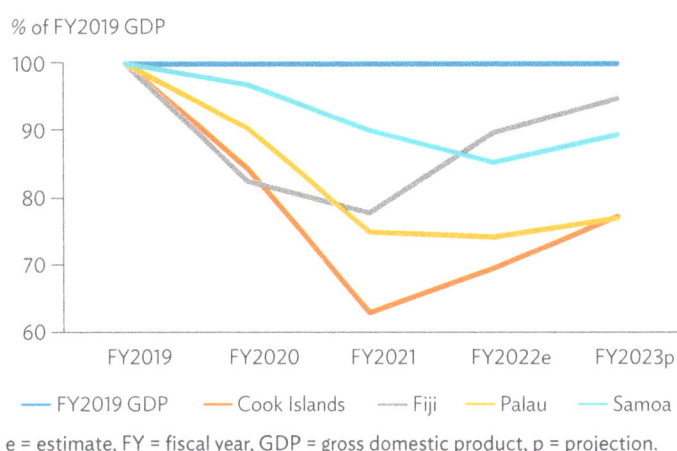

% of FY2019 GDP

FY2019 GDP — Cook Islands — Fiji — Palau — Samoa

e = estimate, FY = fiscal year, GDP = gross domestic product, p = projection.
Note: Fiscal years end on 30 June for the Cook Islands and Samoa; 30 September for Palau; and 31 December elsewhere.
Source: Asian Development Outlook database and estimates.

Figure 2: Fiscal Balances of Tourism-Dependent Pacific Economies, FY2017–FY2022

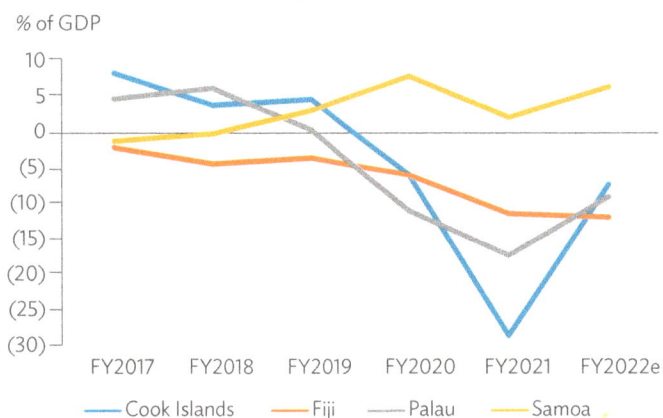

% of GDP

Cook Islands — Fiji — Palau — Samoa

( ) = negative, % = percentage, e = estimates, FY = fiscal year, GDP = gross domestic product.
Note: Fiscal years end on 30 June for the Cook Islands and Samoa; 31 July for Fiji; and 30 September for Palau.
Source: Asian Development Outlook database and estimates.

Beyond the Cook Islands' reliance on tourism, the COVID-19 crisis also underscored vulnerabilities in health-care services, human resource development, the retention of labor, supply chains, and transportation and trade networks. To address these underlying vulnerabilities, the Cook Islands has complemented its immediate recovery efforts with longer-term reforms. In line with the Organisation for Economic Co-operation and Development (OECD) guiding principles for policy coherence for sustainable development, these reforms have focused on principles-based cross-sector actions to manage trade-offs between short and long-term priorities, and between economic, social, and environmental policy goals (Figure 3).[3]

Agile leadership.[4] To moderate the impact of the pandemic on the economy and its citizens, the Government of the Cook Islands recognized that a large fiscal response was required to mitigate economic losses and long-term scarring. The government worked with the private sector and local communities to design a response package to curb economic losses and craft an economic development strategy (EDS) with an accompanying economic recovery roadmap (ERR). These were developed during the peak of the pandemic and enabled the Cook Islands to access grant and debt financing from its development partners to mobilize an exceptional fiscal response needed to mitigate the economic fallout of closed borders.[5] This agile leadership style coordinated action across all levels of government and delivered dramatic increases in cash transfers to businesses, support payments to households, and health spending. The partnership with the private sector also led to innovative tourism marketing campaigns such as the Cook Islands Promise.[6]

A clear strategy and interactive implementation plan. The adoption and implementation of the EDS 2030 and ERR provided the direction for national and external stakeholders to collectively support the Cook Islands on areas of priority.[7] The EDS provides an overarching

framework aligned with the 2030 Sustainable Development Goals while the ERR serves as the main vehicle to drive economic recovery between FY2021 and FY2025. The ERR focuses on growing the Cook Islands GDP back to pre-COVID levels (around NZ$550 million)[8] by 2025 while adhering to fiscal responsibility rules.[9] The main workstreams of the ERR are interlinked and include (i) reducing the cost of borrowing, (ii) managing public debt, (iii) infrastructure investment, (iv) productivity growth, (v) addressing barriers to business performance, (vi) improving public sector efficiency, (vii) labor force and population, and (viii) foreign investment to benefit the Cook Islands. The workstreams promote collaboration between oversight and line agencies in the government and fast-track outstanding reforms such as the review and updating of the medium-term debt strategy. The ERR also helps to improve the government's decision-making mechanisms to manage fiscal risks and direct efforts to improve the effectiveness of the Public Service.

Establishing a governance mechanism to ensure fiscal discipline. To ensure oversight of government finances (including cash and debt management issues) while ensuring key stakeholders are aware of associated risks, the government established a cash management committee comprising senior government officials and development partners. The arrangement was also part of the measures agreed between the government and some development partners (the Government of New Zealand and ADB) to actively monitor fiscal risks and their implications for government cash flows. This mechanism has served as an avenue to strategize on several areas including building cash buffers; assessing options to better manage debt; and strengthening forecasting of revenue, expenditure, and capital spending. The committee actively monitors the implementation of the medium-term fiscal strategy and emergency cash management strategy, both being conditions of ADB precautionary financing.[10] This mechanism also provides a platform to identify and source technical assistance to support certain reforms—where appropriate—and

Figure 3: Guiding Principles for Policy Coherence for Sustainable Development

Inform decision-making, and adjust policies in light of potential negative effects

Systematically **consider the effects of policies** on people's well-being "here and now", "elsewhere" and "later"

Engage all relevant actors to identify challenges, set priorities, align actions and mobilize resources

Align priorities and **promote coordinated action at different levels of government**

Mobilize whole-of-government action and orient policy development toward sustainable development

Support present needs and those of future generations in a balanced manner

Capitalize on synergies and address trade-offs between economic, social and environmental policy areas

Resolve divergences between policies, including between domestic and external policies

Source: OECD. 2020. *OECD Policy Responses to COVID-19: Building a coherent response for a sustainable post-COVID-19 recovery.*

telegraph financing needs to development partners. The setup also helps to increase awareness among departments on fiscal issues requiring tailored solutions and highlights best practices in terms of transparency with development partners on government public finances. This mechanism could also be useful in other smaller island nations for informed and timely decision-making.

Strengthening government functions for effective service delivery. The COVID-19 pandemic highlighted individual and institutional capacity constraints to dealing with complex issues that require cross-sector and interdisciplinary approaches. The limited availability of quality data compounded the challenges faced in identifying appropriate responses needed to address development challenges. Recognizing this—and in line with the workstream on improving the public sector efficiency of the ERR— the government embarked on a functional review to assess the efficiency and effectiveness of public services in the Cook Islands. The review identified policy options to strengthen and improve functions, systems, and structures of the public sector through greater inter-agency collaboration to support more efficient and effective service delivery. The review was seen by the government as a timely exercise to help re-set itself to support an agile workforce that will deliver sustainable development outcomes for the Cook Islands. The findings will be critical in informing the restructuring of business- and change-management processes to support the intended transformation. It will also support the identification of technical assistance needed to support coherent public sector management reforms.

The reforms undertaken by the Cook Islands present a valuable case study of how small island developing states can respond when faced with disasters unprecedented in size and scope. These actions provided the necessary stepping stones to deepen policy dialogue, collaboration, learning, and development that underpinned their integrated approach to managing the COVID-19 shock. While the country still faces a long road to economic recovery and rebuilding fiscal buffers, the decisive and quick actions that were taken have left the economy in a strong position to rebound over the coming years.

Endnotes

[1] 171,713 visitor arrivals in FY2019.

[2] To support the structural transformation and diversification, the Cook Islands has made strides to establish a center of excellence in information and communication technology (ICT) at the University of the South Pacific campus in Rarotonga to create an industry-ready ICT talent pool to boost the financial services industry. Government of the Cook Islands. 2021. *Economic Development Strategy 2030*. Rarotonga.

[3] OECD. 2020. *OECD Policy Responses to COVID-19: Building a coherent response for a sustainable post-COVID-19 recovery.*

[4] A leadership style that strives to remove roadblocks to success so that employees can be more effective and productive. It sharpens focus, accelerates action, and is responsive to groups of people or organizations in complex, uncertain, and rapidly changing environments. P. Behrens. 2022. What is Agile Leadership? *Agile Leadership Journey.* 21 August.

[5] The payments benefited 455 businesses and at least 3,178 employees. Business Grants supported 460 businesses, and Sole Trader Grants supported 174 sole traders. The Government of New Zealand, ADB, and the Asian Infrastructure Investment Bank were the main external financiers during the pandemic.

[6] Cook Islands Tourism Corporation. *Cook Islands Promise.*

[7] Government of the Cook Islands. 2021. *Cook Islands Economic Development Strategy 2030.* Rarotonga; Government of the Cook Islands. 2021. *Economic Recovery Roadmap.* Rarotonga.

[8] Real GDP in 2016 dollars. Government of the Cook Islands, Ministry of Finance and Economic Management. 2022. *Economic Recovery Roadmap: Monitoring Report 2021/22.* Rarotonga.

[9] Government of the Cook Islands. 2021. *Medium-term Fiscal Framework Update.* Rarotonga.

[10] ADB. 2021. *Cook Islands: Supporting Sustainable Economic Recovery Program.* Manila.

References

ADB. Asian Development Outlook Database (accessed 10 July 2023).

ADB. 2021. *Cook Islands: Supporting Safe Recovery of Travel and Tourism Project.*

ADB. 2021. *Proposed Policy-Based Loan and Precautionary Financing Option Load - Cook Islands: Supporting Sustainable Economic Recovery Program.*

P. Behrens. 2022. What is Agile Leadership? *Agile Leadership Journey.* 21 August.

Cook Islands Tourism Corporation. *Cook Islands Promise.* Rarotonga.

Government of the Cook Islands. 2021. *Cook Islands Economic Development Strategy 2030.* Rarotonga.

Government of the Cook Islands. 2021. *Economic Recovery Roadmap.* Rarotonga.

Government of the Cook Islands. 2021. *Primary Healthcare Development Strategy.* Rarotonga.

Government of the Cook Islands. 2022. *Economic Recovery Roadmap: Monitoring Report 2021/22.* Rarotonga.

OECD. 2020. *Policy Responses to COVID-19: Building a coherent response for a sustainable post-COVID-19 recovery.*

United Nations. *Sustainable Development Goals.*

Fiji's new budget: Balancing consolidation and sustainable recovery

Lead authors: Isoa Wainiqolo and Noel Del Castillo

Fiji announced its new national budget for FY2024 (ending 31 July 2024) on 30 June 2023. Boosted by a strong economic recovery, the budget lays out the government's plan to gradually withdraw the pandemic rescue package it mobilized to set a platform for sustainable fiscal and economic recovery. The prolonged impact of the pandemic resulted in a significant rise in Fiji's public debt, as revenues were only half of the pre-pandemic levels and expenditures increased to support vulnerable groups. Public debt increased by 36 percentage points during FY2019–FY2022, one of the largest increases among countries in Asia and the Pacific (Ferrarini et al. 2023). The budget supports the process of fiscal consolidation bringing the fiscal deficit down from 11.9% of GDP in FY2022, to an estimated 6.2% of GDP in FY2023, and 4.8% of GDP in FY2024. The new revenue measures include raising value-added tax (VAT) and corporate tax rates to boost domestic resource mobilization efforts. Major expenditure increases are to support additional staffing needs, superannuation contributions, and increased capital investment in the roads, water, and health sectors.

THE BACKDROP

Before the pandemic, Fiji's fiscal position was already under pressure with the average deficit growing to around 4.0%, during FY2016–FY2020, which was due to weaker revenue collection and exacerbated by the onslaught of several tropical cyclones which strained government resources. The share of indirect and direct taxes to total revenue declined during FY2020–FY2023 to 53% (from 63% during 2014–2019), and to 21% from 25%, as grants and asset sales increased (Figure 4).[1] Revenue performance weakened due to tax policy measures implemented in the years before the pandemic such as the reduction of the VAT rate from 15% to 9%, a higher personal income tax-free threshold, and an increased use of tax incentive schemes (World Bank 2023). In addition, the tax reduction measures introduced in FY2021, as part of the government's COVID-19 support package, resulted in overall revenue loss equivalent to 5.0% of GDP (International Monetary Fund [IMF] 2021). Finally, several tropical cyclones—such as Ian, Pam, Winston, and Harold—have pushed the government to reallocate spending to provide immediate relief to affected citizens and earmark capital resources for reconstruction costs.

As early as 2016, the IMF had expressed the need for fiscal consolidation to better map out the government's medium-to long-term plans and sustainably respond to future shocks. When tropical cyclone Winston hit Fiji in February 2016, it derailed plans for fiscal consolidation as the government responded to damages and losses inflicted that were estimated at F$2 billion. The Government of Fiji mobilized several social protection interventions to respond to the immediate humanitarian needs of affected Fijians. These came in the form of social welfare top-up payments, food voucher programs, housing programs, and emergency access to pension

funds amounting to F$344.7 million (Mansur et al., 2017). The government had to roll out a similar—though significantly larger—response when the pandemic forced the closure of many businesses resulting in a loss of households' livelihood and incomes.

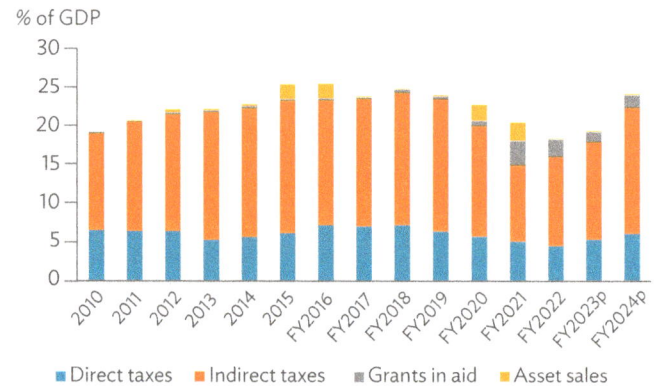

Figure 4: Fiji Major Components of Government Revenue

% of GDP

Direct taxes — Indirect taxes — Grants in aid — Asset sales

FY= fiscal year, GDP = gross domestic product, p=projection.
Note: Starting FY2016, fiscal years end on 31 July of that year.
Source: Government of Fiji. *Budget Estimates*. Suva (15 years: 2010–FY2024).

As climate events and the pandemic wreaked havoc on Fiji, these government responses and interventions have raised the urgency to proceed with the long-planned fiscal consolidation program. In its Article IV Mission in March 2023, the IMF took note of the high government debt—which is equivalent to 85% of GDP—and pointed out how Fiji's high debt ratio clouds the country's prospects despite its strong economic recovery last year.

THE BUDGET

The national budget for FY2024 lays out some of the concrete plans for fiscal consolidation. The government aims to reduce the fiscal deficit from the equivalent of 11.9% of GDP in FY2022 to 6.2% of GDP in FY2023, and further narrow it to 4.8% of GDP in FY2024 (Figure 5). The government is relying on a combination of revenue policy changes, nominal GDP growth, and a recovery in the tax base to offset the increase in expenditures and bring down the debt-to-GDP ratios. While nominal debt is expected to increase up to FY2026, the government is anticipating the debt-to-GDP ratio to fall from 88.2% in FY2022 to 81.2% in FY2023, and 79.3% in FY2024 as GDP grows.

On the revenue side, the government intends to raise the VAT rate to 15% (from 9% and 12.5% for some items) which is expected to increase VAT revenues by 50%, alongside improving economic activity.[2] Corporate tax rates will also be raised from 20% to 25% while departure tax for tourists will be increased gradually.

For expenditures, operating payments are budgeted to increase by 10.9% to cover additional staffing needs and increased superannuation contributions. Total capital expenditures will increase by 23.6% as the government increases spending on roads, water, health, and energy sectors.

Figure 5: Fiji Government Finance

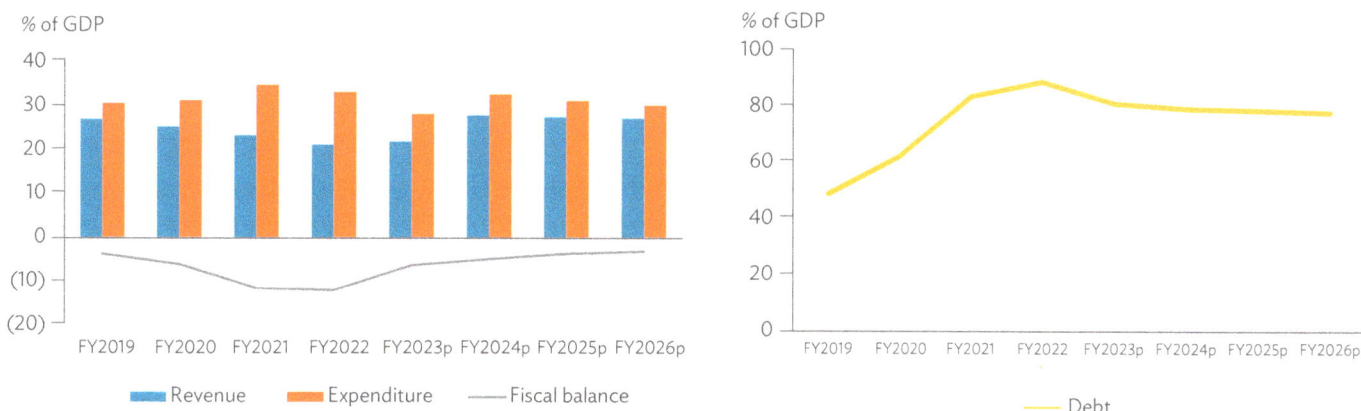

FY= fiscal year, GDP = gross domestic product, p=projection.
Note: Fiscal years end 31 July of that year.
Source: Government of Fiji. *Budget Supplement FY2023–2024*. Suva.

Figure 6: Fiji Annual % Change in Government Finance

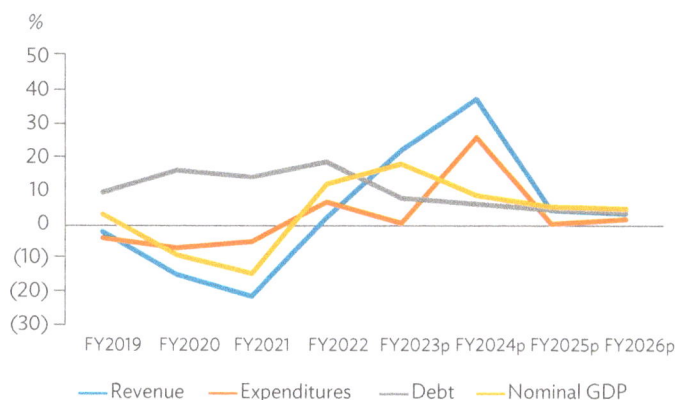

FY= fiscal year, GDP = gross domestic product, p=projection.
Note: Fiscal years end 31 July of that year.
Source: ADB staff computation based on Government of Fiji. *Budget Supplement FY2023–2024*. Suva.

While the intent of the budget is clear, its impact on sustainable economic recovery may be tested. Higher tax rates can be expected to dampen consumer and business demand. Meanwhile, the planned higher expenditure may lead to more imports putting pressure on Fiji's current balance of payments position.

RISKS TO FISCAL CONSOLIDATION AND ECONOMIC OUTLOOK

Fiji's fiscal outlook hinges on continued economic recovery into the medium term. A 26% increase in expenditures in the FY2024 National Budget places heavy pressure on the new revenue measures to meet their targets to avoid wider deficits and put fiscal consolidation plans at risk (Figure 6).

While Fiji is earmarked to record one of the highest growth rates in the Pacific subregion in 2023, fiscal and monetary tightening in major tourism source markets in response to high inflation may adversely affect tourist real discretionary income in the coming months, jeopardizing the revenue recovery. Of the key tourism source markets, Australia and the United States are reportedly facing an economic slowdown, while New Zealand entered a technical recession in the second quarter of the year amid high inflation environment. All central banks have indicated further tightening should inflation remain above target. To sustain tourism recovery, price competitiveness against similar destinations and household disposable incomes in key markets will be important factors in supporting tourism moving forward.

A FINE LINE

Given that not all economic sectors have returned to pre-pandemic performance, raising revenue from corporates may be concentrated on a few sectors such as tourism. While raising indirect taxes such as VAT may boost government revenues, consideration must be given to those in the middle-income group. Only 20,000 workers in Fiji are paying income taxes, with the threshold set at F$30,000 a year (Government of Fiji 2023a). According to the ILO, around 2% of Fijians are earning below $1.90/day in purchasing power parity or are *extremely poor* (ILO 2023).[3] The proportion increases to 16% for the *moderately poor* earning between $1.90 and $3.20 a day, while around 39% are considered *near poor* earning between $3.20 and $5.50 a day. Fiji's national minimum wage rate was set at F$3.01/hour effective 1 April 2022 and was set to increase in stages up to F$4.00/hour by 1 January 2023. Those in this income category may not necessarily be covered under social welfare support and may need to pay more for items outside of the 22 VAT zero-rated list.

The economic recovery is supported by the strong rebound in the tourism industry. While risks are tilted to the downside with the slowdown in major tourist source markets, fiscal consolidation is necessary to support public investment in key areas such as health, education, and water. The new revenue measures are critical but need to be balanced out with a strong social protection system to ensure that the most vulnerable people are protected and that the tourism price competitive edge is somewhat protected. With 24.1% of Fijians living below the poverty line pre-pandemic, raising taxes at a time when the economy has not fully recovered or income levels restored needs to be carefully monitored.

Endnotes

1   This includes the Energy Fiji Limited divestment.

2   To protect low-income earners, a selected 22 items are zero-rated/VAT exempted. This includes basic food items and prescribed medicines with the latter being the new inclusion to the list in this budget.

3   According to the ILO, individuals are considered poor if they live in a household with a daily per capita consumption or income of less than $1.90, believed to be the monetary amount needed to cover the costs of basic food, clothing, and shelter around the world.

References

ADB. ADB COVID-19 Policy Database. (accessed 5 July 2023).

B. Ferrarini, S. Dagli, and P. Mariano. 2023. Sovereign Debt Vulnerabilities in Asia and the Pacific. *ADB Economics Working Paper Series. No. 680.* Manila: Asian Development Bank.

Government of Fiji, Fiji Bureau of Statistics. n.d. *2019–20 Household Income and Expenditure Survey Main Report.* Suva.

Government of Fiji, 2023 Fiji Fiscal Review Committee. 2023a. *Report of the Committee.* Suva.

Government of Fiji, Ministry of Finance, Strategic Planning, National Development and Statistics. 2023b. *Medium Term Fiscal Strategy 2024–2026.* Parliamentary Paper No. 7 of 2023. Suva.

Government of Fiji, Ministry of Finance, Strategic Planning, National Development and Statistics. 2023c. *Economic and Fiscal Update Supplement to the 2023–2024 Budget Address.* Suva.

International Labour Organization (ILO). Statistics on Working Poverty (accessed 27 June 2023).

ILO. 2019. The working poor, or how a job is no guarantee of living conditions. *Spotlight on Work Statistics.* No. 6. April.

International Monetary Fund (IMF). 2021. Republic of Fiji 2021 Article IV Consultation. *IMF Country Report.* No. 21/257. Washington, DC.

2023. IMF Staff Completes 2023 Article IV Mission to Fiji. Press release. No. 23/86. 21 March.

A. Mansur, J. Doyle, and O. Ivaschenko. 2017. Social Protection and Humanitarian Assistance Nexus for Disaster Response: Lessons Learnt from Fiji's Tropical Cyclone Winston. *Discussion Paper.* No. 1701. Washington, DC: World Bank.

World Bank. 2023. *Fiji Public Expenditure Review.* Washington, DC.

Building resilience in Kiribati and Tuvalu through digitalization and e-commerce

Lead authors: Noel Del Castillo, Lily-Anne Homasi, and Isoa Wainiqolo

Weak digital connectivity is a persistent challenge across the Pacific, particularly in the small atoll states of Kiribati and Tuvalu. In many countries, digitalization has catalyzed critical public sector-led initiatives to improve the delivery of service to the people and helped provide opportunities for micro, small, and medium-sized enterprises (MSMEs) in the private sector through e-commerce.[1]

As more consumers engage in online transactions, e-commerce can play an increasingly important role in the global economy which even small island countries could benefit from, provided they improve digital infrastructure, set up regulatory frameworks, and introduce electronic payment solutions. One of the benefits of strong digital connectivity is a thriving e-commerce sector, which became an important driver of growth in many economies during the COVID-19 pandemic, helping businesses survive and flourish by providing an alternative marketplace amid movement restrictions. For these atoll states, e-commerce offers huge potential to support the participation of their economies in international and regional markets, allowing them to build resilience. However, the sudden need to shift to doing business digitally caught many Pacific countries unprepared. It exposed the key constraints to the full adoption of e-commerce, preventing these countries from taking advantage of the potential benefits.

KIRIBATI

Digitalization in Kiribati has improved, yet limited infrastructure remains a key challenge. Kiribati's remoteness has slowed the connection to existing undersea fiber-optic cables.[2] The distance between its islands has made it difficult and expensive to invest in reliable information and communication technology (ICT) network infrastructure. The country's international connectivity is provided only through an international satellite connection for the internet on Tarawa and nearby islands. This offers limited bandwidth capacity and is susceptible to weather disruptions, resulting in unreliable access to ICT services across the country. 4G services are only available in South Tarawa, Abemama, Tabiteuea North, and Onotoa, while 3G services are available in South Tarawa, North Tarawa, Abaiang, Marakei, Maiana, and Kiritimati (United Nations Conference on Trade and Development [UNCTAD] 2019a). People on other islands can access the internet only through Island Council premises. Nonetheless, there have been notable improvements. Internet speed in Kiribati has significantly increased from 100 megabits per second in 2016 to more than 1,200 megabits per second as of November 2020 (Government of Kiribati 2021). The average cost of mobile data fell from $11.10 for 1 gigabyte in 2019 to $3.40 in 2022 (Figure 7). Mobile cellular subscription in the country is around 40 for every 100 people in 2021, below the average of 60 per 100 people for Pacific DMCs. Unique cellular subscriber penetration recorded a huge jump from only 19% of the population in 2018 to 44% in 2022 (GSMA 2023).[3] Internet access has been steadily rising with almost half of the population able to access it during 2019–2021 compared to only an average of one-quarter of the population during 2016–2018 (Figure 8).

The absence of e-payment and cashless solutions is a major bottleneck in the adoption of e-commerce in Kiribati. Another hurdle is the narrow scope of activities associated with lending for business expansion. The basic financial services in the country focus on deposit and withdrawal services, while cash remains the primary mode of payment. Availability of financial services is largely located in South Tarawa and Kiritimati while island councils serve as access points in the outer islands. ANZ Bank is the only commercial bank in Kiribati while Amalgamated Telecom Holdings Kiribati, Ltd. is the only digital financial services provider that offers mobile money solutions. The paucity of e-payment solutions reflects the cost of providing such services. The availability of access to financing designed for MSMEs is important to create an environment that is conducive to e-commerce (UNCTAD 2019a), however access to financing remains a considerable challenge.

Reliable transport infrastructure and sound logistics are key components of a fully functioning e-commerce sector. There is high demand for shipping services and distribution of cargo and supplies for residents of South Tarawa and some isolated islands of Kiribati (UNCTAD 2019a). The movement of goods and people is difficult and costly in Kiribati. Airfreight can provide alternative solutions for the delivery of goods but is expensive. High costs relating to the shipment and clearing of goods have become key barriers to international trade. This is aggravated by the country's issue with its physical address and postcode system, with only 15% of the population able to receive mail at home via postal services (UNCTAD 2019a). With limited shipping options available, postal services provide a crucial and viable alternative to allow the movement of goods.

Weak connectivity and a lack of trust in e-commerce in Kiribati translate into low use of the internet for business purposes. Higher education and training programs have not yet adopted curricula suitable to develop e-commerce skills. Consequently, there are low levels of digitalization and sophistication among MSMEs, impeding them from exploring potential opportunities in e-commerce.[4] Online educational programs at all levels will be vital in propagating digital awareness and literacy. Promoting awareness of cybersecurity to build a safe and secure ICT ecosystem is an important first step in building trust and confidence in e-commerce and encouraging businesses to participate in it.

The legal and regulatory framework that will enable and facilitate e-commerce transactions is not yet in place. There are no laws that recognize the validity of electronic documents and transactions or that govern electronic contracting, which is a necessary underpinning for electronic payments and electronic funds transfer transactions. Laws relating to online consumer protection, financial sector regulatory frameworks, and data privacy have likewise not been put in place. However, the government's National ICT Policy and Investment Policy Framework includes provisions that will aid in the preparation for a data protection and privacy law, an electronic transaction bill, a review of evidence act, and the establishment of internet banking (UNCTAD 2019a). The government also started

working on an electronic transaction bill in 2017 and has sought guidance from the United Nations Commission on International Trade Law to ensure the compatibility of the draft law with international standards (UNCTAD 2019a).

Figure 7: Cost of Mobile Data, 2019–2022

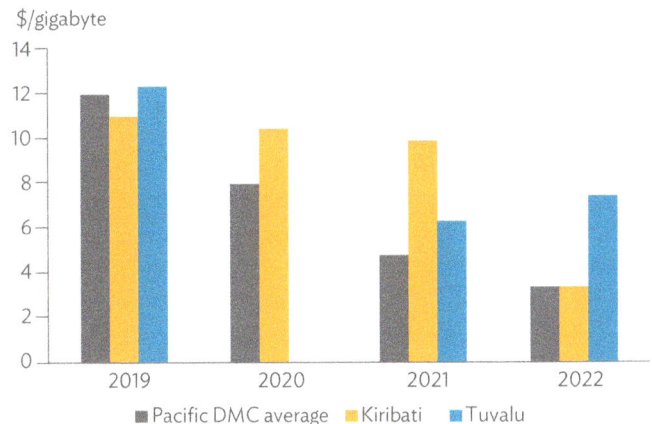

DMC = developing member country.

Note: No data available for Tuvalu in 2020.

Source: Asian Development Bank estimates using Cable.co.uk Worldwide Mobile Data Pricing 2022 (accessed 16 June 2023).

Figure 8: Individuals Using the Internet

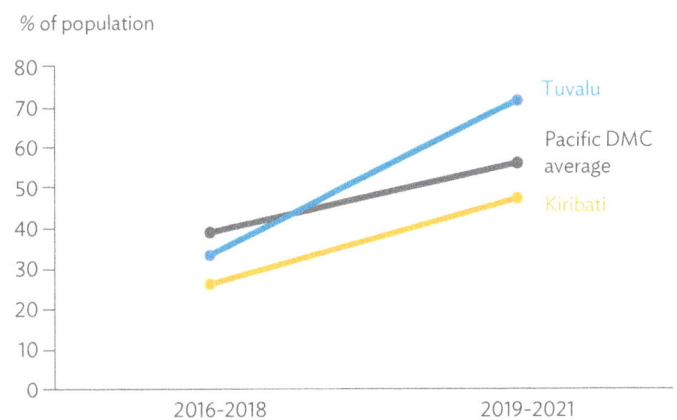

DMC = developing member country.

Note: The average figure does not include the Cook Islands, the Marshall Islands, Niue, and Palau due to the unavailability of data.

Source: Asian Development Bank estimates using World Bank World Development Indicators (accessed 16 June 2023).

TUVALU

Tuvalu's small population and vast distances among the islands have made it costly to deliver ICT services and hindered the development of the sector.[5] Approximately 40% of the population lives on the outer islands, although they represent only about 25% of the total revenue from the ICT market.

Internet access has improved from less than two-fifths of the population being able to access the internet during 2016–2018 to almost three-quarters during 2019–2021 (Figure 8). Although internet users are now higher in Tuvalu than the Pacific DMC average, internet connection remains unreliable for Tuvaluans. Since the introduction of internet broadband services in 2015, Tuvaluans have relied on satellite connection for internet access. While there have been improvements to access, satellite connectivity remains highly dependent on weather conditions. The cost of service has remained one of the highest among Pacific DMCs with an average price of $7.50 for 1 gigabyte of mobile data in 2022, more than 100% above the subregional average price (Figure 7). As of 2023, 3G and 4G services are limited to Funafuti, the capital, although Wi-Fi internet access is available in one location on each of the outer islands. Mobile cellular subscription in Tuvalu is at 80 for every 100 people, but a closer look reveals that unique cellular subscriber penetration is only at 27% of the total population. Tuvalu has a draft ICT policy supported through a public–private partnership between the government, Tuvalu Telecom Corporation, and the World Bank.[6] The project aims to improve telecommunications and internet connectivity to facilitate trade. The policy is expected to guide reforms to boost connectivity in Tuvalu. However, until further improvements to the country's ICT infrastructure are undertaken, costs will remain relatively high, and connectivity will remain low.

Inadequate physical infrastructure and limited domestic and international trade opportunities hamper the development of e-commerce in Tuvalu.[7] With Funafuti as the country's economic hub, economic activity and service delivery in the outer islands are weak. The lack of dedicated logistics solutions for e-commerce is another constraint that hinders investment from the private sector. Inter-island transport depends heavily on marine vessels because many islands are too small for airfields. However, most of the docks are unable to accommodate larger vessels and cannot operate at nighttime due to limited equipment to ensure the safety of passengers and cargo.

The fledging financial sector is another constraint to the development of e-commerce in Tuvalu. Cash is the primary means of payment used in transactions. The absence of basic electronic banking capabilities such as ATMs and credit card facilities increases transaction costs and hampers the development of the private sector, tourism, and trade. The National Bank of Tuvalu is the sole provider of banking services, mainly revolving around deposits, loans, and foreign exchange transactions. For the few consumers and businesses maintaining bank accounts in Australia and New Zealand, e-commerce transactions were facilitated using foreign-issued credit cards. Improving the financial sector will require upgrading facilities and introducing new services, among others.[8] But this should be complemented with adequate training and education, especially because the private sector also has limited information on international payment mechanisms, and electronic and mobile payments. Access to financing remains a significant challenge in Tuvalu, especially for outer island rural communities. Like in Kiribati, access to financing for MSMEs is vital for the development of e-commerce (UNCTAD 2019b). However, the high number of non-performing loans prevents the banking system from fully responding to the lending needs of the private

sector, and access to alternative types of finance is not yet available in the country.

The limited technical know-how of the private sector on e-commerce reflects the gap in the ICT knowledge and skills needed to drive the sector using technology. These constitute some of the primary barriers to the adoption of e-commerce and the increased use of ICT in businesses. Like Kiribati, this is largely because of limited connectivity and a lack of trust (due to limited exposure and other factors) in e-commerce (UNCTAD 2019b). There is a need to provide broader support to explore the digital platform and promote digital literacy in higher education and training programs apart from other important areas such as ICT engineering and basic office software skills. With both governments identifying information technology and ICT skills as a national priority in their medium-term development plan, the private sector could relook at its business development services and include support for digital transformation.

Efforts to further develop e-commerce in Tuvalu would benefit from establishing enabling laws that govern electronic transactions, data protection, and online consumer protection. The development of the legal framework for e-commerce is crucial in supporting the country's nascent digital economy. Although there is already a draft law on cybercrime, adopting a consumer act and other laws will be helpful for both consumers and businesses to gain confidence in adopting e-commerce.

CONCLUSION

Digital technology has played an important role in sustaining economic activity at the height of pandemic lockdowns. As countries emerge from the pandemic and take on the task of improving economic resiliency, accelerating the adoption of digital technology can help improve the long-term prospects of their economies. For Pacific countries like Kiribati and Tuvalu, digitalization through e-commerce can help overcome the development challenges of remoteness from international markets, poor connectivity between and within countries, and lack of economic opportunities. Internet usage has significantly increased for both countries which bodes well for the adoption of e-commerce. However, it needs to address the crucial impediments such as limited digital infrastructure, inadequate transport infrastructure and logistics solutions, weak regulatory frameworks, and a nascent financial sector. These will help hasten the adoption of e-commerce and allow them to enjoy the potential benefits it offers.

Vital reforms are being undertaken at subregional and country levels. Development partners are providing support to improve connectivity in the Pacific. The Asian Development Bank is financing projects that will provide high-quality internet connectivity at a low cost.[9] Both Kiribati and Tuvalu stand to gain from the spread of submarine cable connections which will deliver faster and more reliable internet connectivity. Both governments are actively looking at several key national reform areas that will upgrade infrastructure, develop ICT skills and awareness, expand financial services, and create an enabling legal environment that can encourage consumers and businesses to consider e-commerce. Given the persistence of unique and inherent development challenges that can pose an obstacle to these projects, the collaboration between governments, the private sector, and development partners will be essential to the success of planned reforms and upgrades.

Endnotes

1 E-commerce is defined as the purchase and sale of products (such as physical goods, digital products, or services) transacted over computer networks. Technologies such as internet and electronic data interchange over devices such as personal computers, tablets, and mobile phones can be used for such purposes. E-commerce includes both internet retailing and mobile commerce (ADB 2018).

2 There are efforts to address the digital infrastructure gap through subregional submarine cable projects, although supply-side issues have caused delays in the implementation of the projects.

3 A unique mobile subscriber is a single individual who has subscribed to a mobile service and can hold multiple mobile connections (i.e., SIM cards) (https://www.gsma.com/newsroom/blog/understanding-7-billion-counting-connections-and-people/).

4 A business' stage of development is also a factor for low levels of digitalization and sophistication; many smaller businesses simply have no digital systems supporting their back-office operations.

5 Ironically, a major source of revenue for the Government of Tuvalu comes from the leasing of Tuvalu's country code top-level domain: tv. With around 430,000 domains existing with the suffix TV, the revenue being generated from this rent amounts to 10%–12% of Tuvalu's GDP (UNCTAD 2019b).

6 World Bank. TV: Telecommunications and ICT Development Project. Washington, DC; and World Bank. 2019. Affordable, Faster Connectivity for Tuvalu. Press release. 15 January.

7 Tuvalu has an "e-commerce Tuvalu" social media page marketing Tuvalu products, but challenges remain with the transportation of goods.

8 One of the financial institutions—the Development Bank of Tuvalu—launched its website and social media account in May 2021, providing an alternative means for its clients to access financial services via the digital platform (https://www.developmentbank.tv/).

9 ADB. Regional: Improving Internet Connectivity for Micronesia Project; ADB. Regional: Asia-Pacific Remote Broadband Internet Satellite Project.

References

Asian Development Bank. 2018. *Embracing the E-commerce Revolution in Asia and the Pacific.* Manila.

P. Baker and P. Quiles. 2020. *Pacific Region E-commerce Assessment.* Pacific Islands Forum Secretariat. Suva.

Government of Kiribati, Ministry of Information, Communications, Transport and Tourism Development. 2021. *Kiribati Digital Government Project – Preliminary Environmental and Social Management Plan.* Tarawa.

GSMA. 2019. *The Mobile Economy Pacific Islands 2019.* London.

GSMA. 2023. *The Mobile Economy Pacific Islands 2023.* London.

United Nations Conference on Trade and Development (UNCTAD). 2019a. *Kiribati Rapid eTrade Readiness Assessment.* Geneva.

UNCTAD. 2019b. *Tuvalu Rapid eTrade Readiness Assessment.* Geneva.

Nauru: Debt management amid a pandemic

Lead authors: Prince Cruz and Katherine Passmore

Despite the COVID-19 pandemic, Nauru has significantly reduced its public debt. National government debt declined from A$196 million at the end of FY2020 (ended 30 June 2020) to A$61 million at the end of FY2021 (Figure 9). At the end of FY2020, external debt was A$131 million, while domestic debt was A$64 million.[1] As a ratio of GDP, public debt fell from 105% in FY2020 to 31% in FY2021 and continued a downward trend in FY2022 and FY2023.[2] Although debt is projected to rise to 24% of GDP in FY2024 due to new loans from the Export-Import bank (Eximbank) of Taipei,China, the reduction was in sharp contrast to several neighboring economies whose debts rose significantly from 2020 due to higher spending for pandemic response.[3]

The Nauru debt-to-GDP level used to be among the highest in the Pacific. The high debt levels were the consequence of economic collapse after the depletion of phosphate deposits in the late-1990s, culminating in a sovereign default in 2004.[4] The bulk of the external debt was assumed from the now defunct Republic of Nauru Finance Corporation (RONFIN)—established in 1972 to negotiate loans on behalf of the Government of Nauru—while domestic debt is mostly liabilities (deposit guarantees) arising from the Bank of Nauru liquidation. With the partial resolution of outstanding debt, the ratio of external debt to total debt fell from 67% in FY2020 to 13% in FY2021.

The reduction in Nauru's debt was achieved with the settlement of defaulted yen-denominated bonds. During the 1980s, RONFIN issued yen-denominated bonds ("Samurai" bonds) on behalf of the Government of Nauru. When RONFIN defaulted on these bonds in the 1990s, the national government assumed the debt. Following lengthy negotiations and several court cases, in 2021 the Government of Nauru reached an agreement with Firebird Global Master Fund II Ltd., a major holder of these bonds.[5] Firebird received A$4 million for their Samurai bond holdings.[6]

Figure 9: Nauru Public Debt

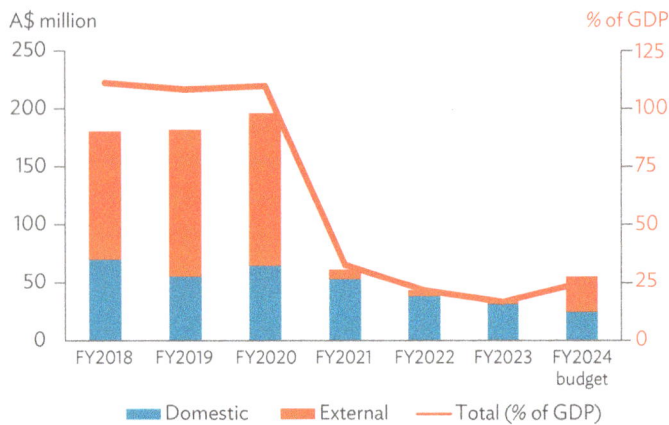

FY = fiscal year, GDP = gross domestic product.
Note: The fiscal year ends on 30 June of the same year.
Source: Government of Nauru. 2023. *2023–2024 Budget Paper No. 1*. Yaren; ADB estimates.

Figure 10: Nauru Revenues and Grants

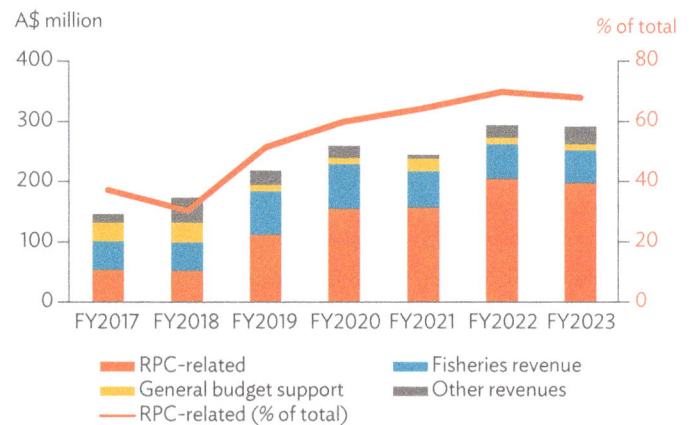

FY = fiscal year, RPC = Regional Processing Center.
Note: The fiscal year ends on 30 June of the same year.
Source: ADB estimates, Nauru budget documents.

The bulk of outstanding debt is domestic, subsumed after the collapse of the Bank of Nauru. Established in 1976, the state-owned Bank of Nauru provided domestic banking services until its closure in 2006. The liability (deposit guarantees) taken on by the Government of Nauru was estimated at A$62.7 million in 2014.[7] When the fiscal situation allows it, the government makes payments to individual depositors and National Phosphate Royalties Trust deposit holders at the Bank of Nauru. The outstanding balance of the liquidation was approximately A$59.5 million in FY2018, falling to A$34.2 million in FY2022.

Despite the debt reduction, Nauru remains unable to access international financial markets. The 2022 debt sustainability analysis by the International Monetary Fund found Nauru's debt to be sustainable, a significant improvement from the unsustainable assessment in 2019. Although Nauru remains unable to access funds on capital markets, since 2018 it has received two loans from the Eximbank of Taipei,China. This includes $5 million for equipment for the Republic of Nauru Phosphate Corporation, and $24.95 million to purchase new aircraft for Nauru Airlines.[8] Repayments for the Nauru Airlines loan will be met through budget support from Taipei,China.

Debt repayment was made possible with continued revenues related to the Regional Processing Centre (RPC).[9] The Nauru economy was not affected significantly by the pandemic. Although economic growth slowed, a contraction was avoided due to higher government spending. The spending was mainly enabled by RPC revenue, which accounted for almost 70% of revenues and grants in FY2022–FY2023 (up from 34% in FY2017–FY2018). In nominal terms, RPC-related revenues grew from an average of A$53 million in FY2017–FY2018 to A$201 million in FY2022–FY2023 (Figure 10). The increase is in line with the RPC transition to "enduring capability," reflecting a memorandum of understanding between the Government of Nauru and the Government of Australia to maintain RPC capability.[10]

With significant uncertainty on the future of the RPC, Nauru has adopted several initiatives to manage debt sustainability. Part of the revenue from RPC is being set aside in the Nauru Intergenerational Trust Fund, which was established in 2015 to contribute to Nauru's long-term self-reliance. With contributions and support from ADB and the governments of Australia, New Zealand, and Taipei,China, total contributions to the trust fund were A$221 million in March 2023, while the investment value of the fund was A$280 million (Figure 11). Further, the Government of Nauru has adopted fiscal responsibility ratios and a Medium-Term Debt Strategy 2023–28.[11]

Figure 11: Nauru Intergenerational Trust Fund Contributions and Investment Value

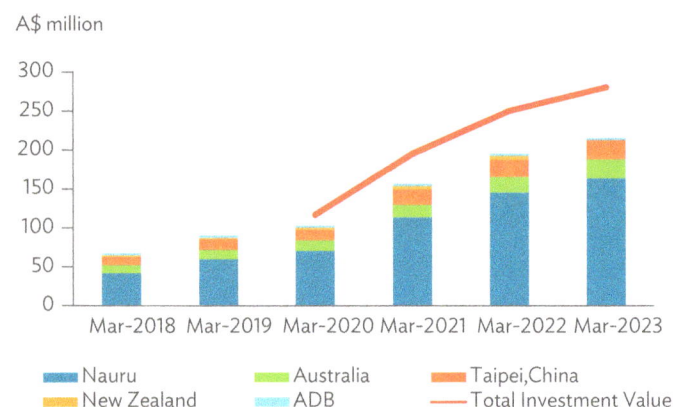

ADB = Asian Development Bank.
Source: Government of Nauru. 2023. *2023–2024 Budget Paper No. 1*. Yaren.

Other initiatives to broaden the economic base include the Nauru Port project and Nauru Airlines' hopper flights to the North Pacific. The country's first all-weather wharf became operational in September 2022 with the project expected to be fully completed by 2024. The facility is expected to attract business and investment opportunities such as tuna docking and processing. After winning the first tender for Australia's Pacific Flights Program, Nauru Airlines resumed flights to Fiji, Kiribati, the Marshall Islands, and the Federated States of Micronesia in October 2022. Under the program, Australia is subsidizing air links from Australia (through Brisbane) to the North Pacific.[12] The flights are expected to boost tourism and trade to Nauru and the North Pacific. Nauru Airlines is also providing support services to neighboring country airlines as they encounter problems in terms of aircraft and crew.

Endnotes

[1] The value of external debt prior to resolution is subjective with the International Monetary Fund (IMF) placing it at A$48.8 million in FY2019 and A$51.4 million in FY2020. Sources: Government of Nauru. 2022. *2022–2023 Budget Paper No. 1.* Yaren; IMF. 2022. *Republic of Nauru: Staff Report for the 2021 Article IV Consultation.* IMF Country Report No. 22/28. Washington, DC.

[2] Some estimates place total debt as a share of GDP at the end of FY2020 up to 114%.

[3] In the Pacific, Fiji and Palau saw the highest debt increases. B. Ferrarini, S. Dagli, and P. Mariano. 2023. Sovereign Debt Vulnerabilities in Asia and the Pacific. *ADB Economics Working Paper Series.* No. 680. Manila: Asian Development Bank.

[4] R. Rajah. 2017. *Securing Sustainability: Nauru's New Intergenerational Trust Fund and Beyond.* Manila: ADB.

[5] IMF. 2022. *Republic of Nauru: Staff Report for the 2021 Article IV Consultation.* IMF Country Report No. 22/28. Washington, DC.

[6] Debt negotiations and resolution were supported by ADB through technical assistance project (TA) 9760: *Improving Pacific Public Financial Management Facility.*

[7] IMF. 2022. *Republic of Nauru: Staff Report for the 2021 Article IV Consultation.* IMF Country Report No. 22/28. Washington, DC.

[8] IMF. 2022. *Republic of Nauru: Staff Report for the 2021 Article IV Consultation.* IMF Country Report No. 22/28. Washington, DC.

[9] The RPC is an Australian facility in Nauru for processing asylum seekers.

[10] ADB. 2023. Central Pacific Economies in *Asian Development Outlook.* April. Manila.

[11] The ratios are i) budget balance must be positive as a share of GDP; ii) personnel as a proportion of current expenditure must be below 30%; and iii) fiscal cash buffer of 2 months adjusted non-RPC expenditure.

[12] Air Niugini won the other tender, connecting Brisbane to Palau through Port Moresby. Sources: G. Johnson. 2022. Nauru Airlines wins Australian tender, will resume north Pacific service. *Radio New Zealand.* 3 October; L. Lewis. 2023. New Pacific air route lands in Palau. *Radio New Zealand.* 1 March.

Managing Niue's prolonged recovery amid volatile fuel costs

Lead author: Isoa Wainiqolo

The Niuean economy contracted by 4.7% in 2020 and 6.2% in 2021 as prolonged border closures stalled tourism and slowed public investment spending. Tourism was the most significant growth driver before the pandemic, with revenues equivalent to about a third of annual GDP. Around 11,000 visitors arrived in Niue per year before 2020, more than 6 times the resident population. While economic activity has improved since borders reopened in June 2022, the single weekly flight is hindering a quick recovery with a second flight only expected to resume in November 2023.

Niue's budget is financed through a combination of domestic revenues (almost one-third of on-budget expenditures) and direct budget support from New Zealand and other donors. The impact of the pandemic on economic activity and revenue collections necessitated a deviation from the government's balanced budget policy. Recurrent spending in FY2021 (ended 30 June) and FY2022 was focused on COVID-19 impact mitigation measures, including government wage subsidies and support to local businesses.

In FY2021, the Government of Niue posted a fiscal deficit equivalent to 17.2% of 2021 GDP as recurrent expenditures were boosted to deal with the pandemic (Figure 12).[1] Development partner revenue, especially from the Government of New Zealand, which averaged 25.4% of GDP helped ease the fiscal burden during this period. The fiscal deficit peaked at 26.4% of GDP in FY2023 and is projected to subside slightly to 23.0% of GDP in FY2024 as revenue outcomes improve.

To support a return to a more balanced fiscal position, a careful examination of public expenditures may be needed. One important element of this evaluation is to look at the sustainability and cost of current fuel subsidy arrangements. In its September 2022 fuel price assessment, the government indicated that high fuel prices over the preceding four months cost NZ$2.6 million in subsidies and cautioned that it may not be able to sustain such levels of spending given post-pandemic economic constraints. The subsidy cost, if annualized, equates to around 31% of total recurrent expenses. Some of these pressures may ease in the coming year due to an easing in global fuel prices, however, the fuel subsidy as of 2023 is likely to continue placing significant pressure on budget sustainability.

There are several options to help reduce fuel subsidy costs in the medium term. Based on the latest available data, Niue's fuel imports cost NZ$3.3 million in 2021 equivalent to 16.7% of total imports, a 3.4% annual increase. Rationalizing fuel subsidies would not only ease the fiscal burden on the government but also serve as an impetus and a means toward greater renewable energy adoption. Only 14% of electricity was generated from renewable energy sources in 2019 and the government targets to increase this share to 80% by 2025. While the renewable energy transition requires significant capital investment by the government and Niue's development partners, part of the costs could be defrayed by potential savings from reduced fuel subsidies. This can help allow for a return to balanced budgets, which will be critical for decoupling the economy from global oil markets and building resilience to future adverse events, including disasters triggered by natural hazards.

Figure 12: Niue Fiscal Balance

% of GDP

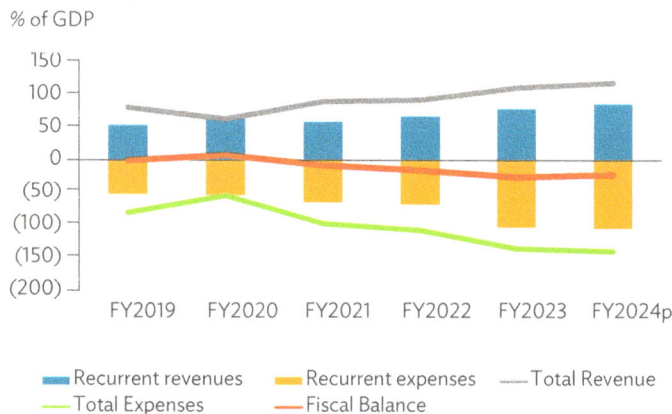

FY = fiscal year, GDP = gross domestic product, p = projection.

Note: Fiscal years end on 30 June of that year.

Source: Government of Niue.

Endnote

[1] Niue's latest GDP release is only up to calendar year 2021. Unless otherwise stated, all fiscal ratios are calculated as a % of 2021 GDP level. Projections for outer years are constrained by the lack of detailed data.

References

Government of Niue. 2020. *Niue PEFA Performance Report 2020*. Alofi.

Government of Niue. 2022. Government of Niue Continues To Subsidise Fuel to Offset Increases. *Media Release*. 8 September. Alofi.

Government of Niue. 2022. Government of Niue Is To Maintain Petrol and Gas Prices at Current Levels. Media release. 10 November. Alofi.

Government of Niue. 2023. *Budget Statement 2023–2024*. Statement by the Minister of Finance, Infrastructure, and Public Service for the introduction of the Budget Estimates 2023/2024 to the Niue Assembly Meeting. 7 June.

Pathways to reclaiming lost ground in the North Pacific

Lead authors: Remrick Patagan, Rommel Rabanal, and Cara Tinio

Like their Pacific peers, the Federated States of Micronesia (FSM), the Republic of the Marshall Islands, and Palau each registered significant economic and social losses due to the COVID-19 pandemic. Extended border closures delayed community transmission of the virus until 2022 and high vaccination rates minimized the resulting waves of cases. However, prolonged isolation—the FSM and the Marshall Islands had among the longest border closures globally, lasting from March 2020 to September 2022—disrupted trade and tourism flows, along with movements of labor and equipment that, in turn, stalled major construction projects. The resulting losses in GDP translate into net economic contractions during FY2020 (ended 30 September 2020 for all three North Pacific economies) to FY2022 of 2.9% in the FSM; 1.6% in the Marshall Islands; and a severe 27.8% in the Palau tourism-driven economy.

LONG ROADS TO RECOVERY

Although the FSM and the Marshall Islands have returned to growth—with Palau slated to join them in the near term—it is critical to underscore that this does not mean that they can immediately recover the losses brought on by the pandemic. For instance, the outlook is clouded by a possible escalation of the impacts of the Russian invasion of Ukraine, which has already fueled inflation (ADB, 2022). Full recovery toward the pre-pandemic growth path can only be achieved through a sustained acceleration in economic growth. If the North Pacific countries only manage to revert to their long-term historical growth rates of 1%–2%, GDP levels—and therefore per capita incomes—will permanently remain below their pre-pandemic paths.

Even with the projected near-term recovery in FY2023 and FY2024, followed by a reversion to long-term growth trends by FY2025 onward, the post-COVID-19 levels of real GDP in the North Pacific economies (shown by the orange dotted lines in Figure 13) will persistently remain below their respective levels under a counterfactual historical growth scenario. They would have grown steadily from FY2020 onward (blue lines) if the COVID-19 shock had not occurred. Gaps can be closed by accelerations above the historical trends, including by implementing a broad suite of growth-enhancing reforms. For example, simulations show that if the North Pacific economies can successfully raise long-term GDP growth performance by 1 percentage point beginning in FY2028 (green lines), each can catch up to the historical growth scenario, albeit after varying intervening periods.

A smaller cumulative contraction in the FSM, coupled with expectations of a relatively strong near-term rebound, can help the economy revert to its pre-pandemic trend by FY2030. The Marshall Islands may be in a similar situation by FY2036. However, the severe impacts of a prolonged economic decline and delayed tourism recovery in Palau suggest a longer road to full recovery, which may not be seen until FY2053. Stronger improvements in long-term economic performance will progressively advance timelines to full recovery.

Figure 13: Growth Simulations for the North Pacific Economies

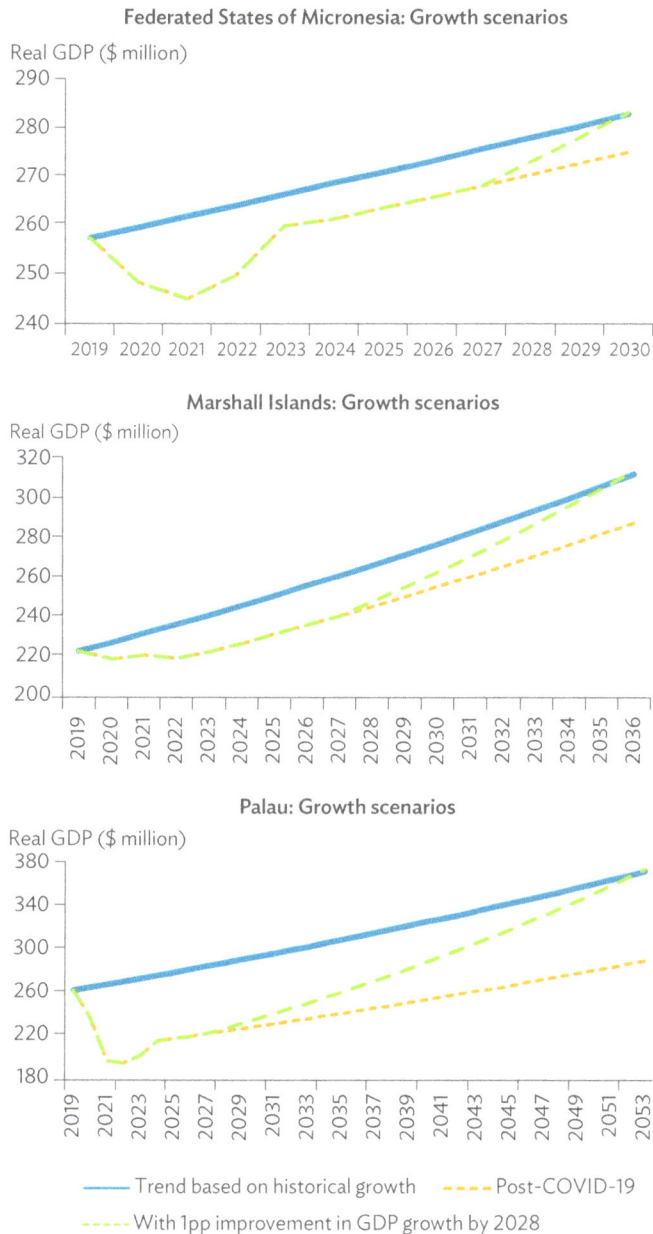

Federated States of Micronesia: Growth scenarios

Marshall Islands: Growth scenarios

Palau: Growth scenarios

— Trend based on historical growth   - - - Post-COVID-19
- - - With 1pp improvement in GDP growth by 2028

COVID-19 = coronavirus disease, GDP = gross domestic product, pp = percentage point.
Note: Years are fiscal years ending 30 September for all three North Pacific economies.
Source: ADB estimates.

PATHWAYS TO SWIFTER RECOVERY

How then can the North Pacific economies accelerate long-term growth? The impending substantial expansion in available fiscal resources through anticipated extensions of each country's Compact of Free Association with the United States—which provides substantial financial assistance and an open migration policy, while allowing the US access to geopolitically important airspace and waters—offers a timely opportunity to improve growth performance toward more inclusive and resilient development.

In January 2023, the Marshall Islands and Palau signed memoranda of understanding (MOUs) for extensions of their existing Compacts, which will significantly increase financial assistance from the US. This was followed by a similar MOU between the FSM and the US in February. In May, both the FSM and Palau secured Compact Review Agreements with the US; negotiations with the Marshall Islands are ongoing. The agreement with Palau reportedly doubles assistance to $889 million in the coming 20 years compared to the previous 2 decades. The FSM had earlier announced consensus on providing for continued economic assistance, increased sector grants to an annual $140 million (or $2.8 billion over 20 years), and a $500 million funding infusion into the FSM Compact Trust Fund spread over 2 years. The agreements will be submitted for approval by the respective Congresses of the FSM, Palau, and the US.

To translate expanded fiscal resources into improved development outcomes, more efficient systems and strengthened implementation capacities—particularly for using compact infrastructure grants—are required. Steps should be supported and sustained to address understaffing and lack of specific technical skills in project management offices, ensure compliance with US building codes and standards, and continuously update development planning and programming practices. These could include sustained capacity building and supplementation support for project management offices from development partners, along with more flexible and differentiated approaches to project implementation tailored to the small island developing state context. Building up institutions and capacity will be indispensable to effective infrastructure planning, prioritization, and maintenance. It is also crucial to these countries' ability to appropriately respond to complex structural challenges such as climate change as well as maximizing available financing in this area (ADB, 2022).

Strengthening project implementation and absorptive capacities can provide additional economic stimulus by raising the contribution of gross fixed capital formation to overall growth. During the decade from FY2010–FY2019, gross fixed capital formation contributed about −1.0 percentage points to overall GDP growth in the FSM, 2.9 percentage points in the Marshall Islands, and 1.4 percentage points in Palau. Raising these by at least 1 percentage point or more could expedite the North Pacific economies' full recovery of losses from the pandemic. The resulting efficiency gains enabled by improved infrastructure could contribute to enhancing long-run growth prospects, potentially opening even shorter paths to full recovery by catching up to projected GDP levels under the historical growth scenario.

Other growth-enhancing reforms would also help facilitate recovery in the North Pacific. Strengthening public financial management enhances overall government efficiency, helping ensure that public investment projects are implemented (i) on time, realizing their maximum economic benefits; and (ii) within budget, freeing up resources that could be channeled toward building fiscal buffers against socioeconomic shocks.

Higher debt burdens and rising debt servicing costs left by the pandemic's macro-fiscal impacts also demand greater efficiency in government expenditure. Among other measures, tariff; financial management; and corporate governance reforms can contribute to improving the quality of public spending by helping reduce needs for periodic transfers to state-owned enterprises. Palau is undertaking policy and legislative reforms to modernize taxation, improve fiscal discipline, and promote private sector activity. Palau is also strengthening the policy and institutional framework for public–private partnerships (PPPs) to support greater private sector participation in public service delivery.

Empirical results derived from panel data of 19 developing economies from Asia and the Pacific suggest that a 1 percentage point increase in the ratio of PPP investment to GDP is correlated with a 0.1 percentage point rise in real per capita GDP growth, with increasing positive effects with higher ratios of PPP investment (Lee et al., 2018).[1] This illustrates that private sector development reforms can be a key component of a broad strategy to gradually raise long-term economic growth performance.

Improvements to infrastructure could be complemented by other enhancements to physical connectivity that would broaden access to livelihood opportunities and essential social services. Harnessing digital connectivity can boost productivity and wages, improve labor participation and employment prospects for women workers, and inform decision-making and market access (Hjort and Sacchetto, 2022).[2] Increased mobile access has been estimated to contribute 0.11% a year to GDP growth in low-income countries (Gruber and Koutroumpis, 2011) and increasing internet use by 1.0 percentage point has been correlated with a 4.3-percentage point boost in exports (Koutroumpis, 2019). Bridging the digital divide also has the potential to promote financial inclusion.

Investing in human capital would build—out of the predominantly young population—an adequate, sustainable supply of labor capable of maximizing potential socioeconomic gains. Investing in primary education is estimated to yield 24.5% in private returns and 17.1% in social returns in middle-income countries such as the FSM, the Marshall Islands, and Palau (Psacharopoulos and Patrinos, 2018). The FSM and the Marshall Islands are working to improve the quality of basic education through better teacher training and student assessments, greater access to teaching and learning resources, and improved school management and community engagement. Such efforts pave the way for other interventions, including increasing access of youth to productive employment and livelihood opportunities. These efforts are also necessary if the North Pacific economies hope to bridge gaps in technical skills and expertise common across small island countries, although addressing this would require more specific interventions beyond broad human capital investments.

CONCLUDING REMARKS

Despite improved growth prospects after the easing of constraints on trade and tourism flows, the North Pacific economies still face a long recovery. Sustained acceleration in economic growth is key to recovering losses from the COVID-19 pandemic; reverting to long-term historical growth rates will not be enough to return to pre-pandemic growth

trajectories. The possibility of increased development assistance under renewed Compacts with the US would provide a significant boost in this regard, but more efficient systems and implementation capacities will be required to capitalize on these resources.

Such enhancements would not only boost near-term stimulus from infrastructure projects but also advance their efficiency-enhancing impacts on the broader economy. Other growth-enhancing reforms to further improve government efficiency—as well as promote connectivity and develop human capital—will be essential to gradually reclaim lost development gains.

Endnotes

[1] The only Pacific DMC included in the study is Fiji.

[2] Internet adoption increases labor force participation (Bahia et al., 2020; Dutz et al., 2012) and enables job search (Viollaz and Winklers, 2020) of women in developing countries. In the case of Viet Nam, it increases demand for female workers ostensibly due to the rise of industries that require skills for which women may have comparative advantage (Chun and Tang, 2018).

References

Asian Development Bank (ADB). Improving the Quality of Basic Education in the North Pacific Project.

ADB. Palau: Recovery through Improved Systems and Expenditure Support Program (Subprogram 1).

ADB. Palau: Recovery through Improved Systems and Expenditure Support Program (Subprogram 2).

ADB. 2022. *Pacific Economic Monitor.* pp. 6–9. Manila. August.

ADB. 2023. *Asian Development Outlook April 2023.* Manila.

K. Bahia et al. 2020. The welfare effects of mobile broadband internet: evidence from Nigeria. *World Bank Policy Research Working Paper 9230.* May.

N. Chun and H. Tang. 2018. Empowered female workers? Firm-level evidence from Viet Nam. *ADB Economics Working Paper Series.* Manila.

M. Dutz et al. 2017. Economywide and sectoral impacts on workers of Brazil's internet rollout. *World Bank Policy Research Working Paper 8042.* April.

H. Gruber and P. Koutroumpis. 2011. Mobile telecommunications and the impact on economic development. *Economic Policy.* 26(67). pp. 387, 389–426. July.

J. Hjort and C. Sacchetto. 2022. Can internet access lead to improved economic outcomes? *World Bank Digital Development.* 5 April.

P. Koutroumpis. 2019. What is the impact of investing in connectivity? British International Investment Impact Study No. 004. London. 28 August.

M. Lee et al. 2018. Deriving Macroeconomic Benefits from Public-Private Partnerships in Developing Asia. *ADB Economics Working Paper Series.* No. 551. Manila: Asian Development Bank.

G. Psacharopoulos and H. A. Patrinos. 2018. Returns to Investment in Education: A Decennial Review of the Global Literature. *World Bank Policy Research Working Paper.* No. 8402. Washington, DC.

M. Viollaz and H. Winklers. 2020. Does the internet reduce gender gaps?: The case of Jordan. *World Bank Policy Research Working Paper 9183.* March.

Policy reform plans and brighter spots on the horizon: Can Papua New Guinea embark on a new sustainable and inclusive growth path?

Lead authors: Marcel Schroder and Magdelyn Kuari

The economic growth of Papua New Guinea (PNG) has been volatile and linked to foreign direct investment in the resource sector and to commodity price fluctuations. During 2015–2020, overall growth averaged 2.8%, driven by the extraction of natural resources such as gold and liquefied natural gas (LNG). Non-resource sector growth averaged only 0.7%. Because annual population growth exceeded 3%, the living standard of the average Papua New Guinean likely declined during this period.

Growth has been held back by many factors. These include a fall in commodity prices; the absence of any major new mineral sector investments; drought and frost in 2015–2016; an earthquake in 2018; the closure of the Porgera gold mine in 2020; the COVID-19 pandemic in 2020 and 2021; and foreign exchange (forex) constraints that have persisted since 2015. In 2021, the economy barely grew at 0.1% before rebounding to 3.2% in 2022. Employment contracted in the non-resource sector on average by 2.2% during 2015–2021 while public debt rose from the equivalent of 29.9% of GDP in 2015 to 48.9% in 2022.

The poor economic performance of PNG reflects its narrow economic base. While the resource sector will continue to drive future growth, PNG needs to diversify its economy and better manage economic cycles to promote sustainable, inclusive growth. Several issues need to be addressed. These include low government revenue collections, a surging wage bill, weak governance, an overvalued exchange rate, and forex restrictions.

The government intends to embark on a reform agenda to address several macroeconomic policy issues which will be aided by an International Monetary Fund (IMF) program approved in March 2023. This follows a request by the Government of Papua New Guinea for a special drawing rights of 684.3 million (equivalent to $918.3 million) budget support loan tied to governance conditions over 38 months. Reforms will focus on (i) strengthening debt sustainability through a multi-year fiscal consolidation program while creating fiscal space to meet critical social needs; (ii) strengthening the mandate and autonomy of the Bank of Papua New Guinea (BPNG), (iii) alleviating forex shortages, and transition to a market-clearing exchange rate; and (iv) operationalizing the Independent Commission Against Corruption (ICAC). PNG will need to meet the program's benchmark targets to fully draw down the loan. The first $310 million was released to PNG in April 2023, and subsequent batches will follow in 2024 and 2025.

STRENGTHENING DEBT SUSTAINABILITY THROUGH FISCAL CONSOLIDATION

The fiscal deficit of PNG surged to 8.9% of GDP amid the pandemic and the closure of the Porgera mine in April 2020 (Figure 14). Since then, the deficit has gradually declined to 6.8% of GDP in 2021 and 5.4% in 2022 and is projected at 4.4% in 2023. The debt-to-GDP ratio rose significantly from under 30.0% in 2013 to 52.2% in 2021 and decreased to 49.8% in 2022. In 2022, there was a fiscal resource revenue windfall of K4.0 billion because of the commodity price spike following the Russian invasion of Ukraine. However, the sovereign wealth fund (SWF) is not yet operational and instead of accumulating savings through deposits, the windfall was allocated to additional expenditure.

The government has committed to a fiscal consolidation path to achieve a fiscal surplus by 2027, which will lead the debt-to-GDP ratio to fall below 50% by 2026. According to the IMF Debt Sustainability Analysis in September 2022, PNG remains at a "high" risk of external and overall debt distress, due mainly to the effects of the COVID-19 pandemic on government revenues and rising external debt. However, the IMF considers external and overall debt to be sustainable provided PNG successfully pursues fiscal consolidation and uses conservative financing strategies.

Figure 14: Papua New Guinea Fiscal Performance and Outlook

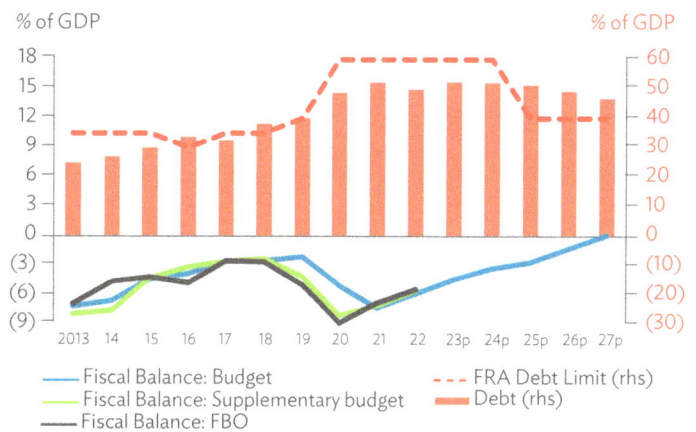

FBO = final budget outcome, FRA = Fiscal Responsibilities Act, GDP = gross domestic product, p = projection, rhs = right-hand scale.

Source: Government of Papua New Guinea, Department of Treasury.

During 2018–2021, the average revenue growth was 4.7%, while the average expenditure growth was 11.6%. The public sector wage bill remains a particular area of concern: its share of government revenue averaged 51% during 2019–2021, diverting spending away from investment projects and essential social needs in health, education, and law and order.

To support the government's fiscal consolidation plan, the IMF program comprises a set of quantitative and indicative targets. In 2023, these include limiting the present value of new external borrowing to $1.405 billion, the fiscal deficit not exceeding K4.985

billion (equivalent to 4.3% of GDP), non-resource tax revenue collection being at least K12.558 billion (10.8% of GDP), and social expenditure not falling below K3.866 billion (3.4% of GDP). The program also seeks to improve revenue collections and expenditure control by implementing the Tax Administration Act and introducing amendments to the Income Tax Act to Parliament by the end of 2023. The IMF program requires the government to enact a new medium term revenue strategy by the end of August 2023 to replace the previous Medium Term Revenue Strategy 2018–2022. Expenditure reforms to improve payroll budgeting include the implementation of the 2022 Staffing Establishment Review for central agencies by conducting human resource business process workshops.

ADDRESSING FOREIGN EXCHANGE SHORTAGES

The PNG economy has grappled with forex shortages since the end of the commodities supercycle in 2014. Although the BPNG has allowed some nominal depreciation, it has resisted full adjustment, instead managing the shortage by rationing forex. In practice, the central bank has controlled the exchange rate through a trading band (75 basis points around the inter-bank market rate) and "moral suasion" since July 2014. Estimates of exchange rate overvaluation range from 13% to 26% (Davies and Schroder 2022; IMF 2023). As a result, there is a sizable backlog of forex orders, estimated at various points in time in the range of $0.3 billion to $1.5 billion. In addition, households and firms likely hold kina assets on their balance sheets that they would like to convert to forex but do not bring to the market. They probably also have latent demand for imported goods and services. This implies that the total backlog is substantially larger than what is visible in the banking system.

In 2022, reserves were supported by external borrowing and the surge in commodity prices following the Russian invasion of Ukraine, reaching $4.1 billion (equivalent to 11.2 months of imports) by year-end. BPNG still only sells about $100 million per month to domestic banks. In early 2023—as commodity prices subsided and the closure of the Porgera mine continued—the forex situation tightened again with increases in average processing time for forex orders and a backlog on commercial bank order books. The situation affected fuel supplies. In January 2023, domestic flights were suspended for 2 days because of a fuel shortage. In February, fuel rationing by Puma Energy closed many service stations and generated long queues outside others. In March, leading PNG business executives in a yearly survey once again identified the lack of forex as the number one impediment to their operations.

Under the IMF program, the government is expected to develop a roadmap by the end of August 2023 and implement—with IMF support—reforms to exchange rate operations and a gradual move to a market-clearing exchange rate. Reform targets include (i) setting a floor on BPNG forex intervention to help reduce pent-up demand for forex and sterilize excess liquidity; (ii) setting a floor on the stock of net foreign exchange reserve; (iii) setting a ceiling on the BPNG gross credit to government, effective throughout the program to avoid monetary deficit financing; and (iv) revising the Central Bank Act to promote BPNG independence, transparency, accountability, and governance.

ENHANCING GOVERNANCE AND OPERATIONALIZING THE ANTICORRUPTION FRAMEWORK

While PNG has comprehensive laws and institutions in place, governance remains weak compared with other regional economies. The capacity of government agencies to implement reform measures is constrained by weak management and technical expertise, limited financial resources, and inadequate performance management. Although there have been some improvements in public financial management, government agencies still need strengthening and capacity development, particularly when it comes to procurement, payroll management, and subnational public financial management systems to control expenditure. Fiscal and debt management remains a central challenge and the government needs to increase the transparency and frequency of fiscal reporting, including reporting debt liabilities.

The IMF program will support efforts by the government in appointing the commissioner and two deputy commissioners for the office of the ICAC as well as recruiting staff for operational functions and providing them with training. Other structural reforms include specifying regulatory processes of the ICAC law and information sharing across relevant entities by the end of 2023.

The program will also support efforts by the government to improve transparency in financial and fiscal data reporting. A particular focus will be on public procurement through the disclosure of information on COVID-19-related procurements by the end of December 2023. In addition, the Treasury seeks to improve the coverage and frequency of budget presentation, while BPNG will improve the production of the financial soundness indicators and resume the timely publication of its audited financial statements.

ADB supports government efforts to improve the operational and financial performance of state-owned enterprises (SOEs) to enhance their financial sustainability. Another focus is on strengthening governance and augmenting transparency, for example, through clearing the backlog of SOE audited financial reports and implementing transparent recruitment processes. The SOE reforms also aim to promote gender equality. These include increasing the representation of women on SOE boards, strengthening reporting on gender indicators, and carrying out gender analysis on new investments in essential services.

ECONOMIC OUTLOOK

The PNG economy in 2023 stands at a crossroads. After almost a decade of economic downturn, there is the prospect of a turnaround. The recovery from the COVID-19 pandemic is underway and the new IMF program promises to support the government in tackling long-lasting macroeconomic policy issues—such as the lack of forex—that have been choking growth. The start of construction of the Papua LNG project in 2024 is also expected to support the near-term outlook. Direct jobs during the construction phase will create more employment and spending in the local economy through multiplier effects, providing a boost to tax revenue. Part of the $12 billion investment volume will flow into the country via financial channels, helping clear pent-up demand in the forex market. Additional adjustments in the exchange rate might be needed to fully restore currency convertibility, which is a necessary condition for the economy to embark on a sustainable growth path that benefits all Papua New Guineans.

PNG also needs to manage revenues stemming from the Papua LNG project to support fiscal consolidation efforts under the IMF program. The created fiscal space will be crucial for future potential disaster relief and climate adaptation programs. Operationalizing the SWF will be key to improving revenue management and enhancing macroeconomic stability to safeguard the economy against shocks, and now is an opportune time to do it. Tax revenue from the resource sector is anticipated to rise in the coming years from the PNG LNG project when tax exemptions expire in 2026, early revenues from Papua LNG when production commences (in 2027 or 2028), and the Porgera mine reopening. In the absence of successful policy reform efforts, there is the danger of a renewed economic stagnation period in the aftermath of the brief boom during the Papua LNG project construction.

References

M.H. Davies and M. Schroder. 2022. A Simple Model of Internal and External Balance for Resource-Rich Developing Countries. *ADB Economics Working Paper Series.* No. 660. Manila: Asian Development Bank.

International Monetary Fund. 2023. *Papua New Guinea: Requests for an Arrangement under the Extended Credit Facility and an Extended Arrangement under the Extended Fund Facility-Press Release; Staff Report; and Statement by the Executive Director for the Papua New Guinea.*

Rebuilding and rehiring: An update on post-COVID-19 tourism in Samoa and Tonga

Lead author: James Webb

The development of tourism in the South Pacific was a key economic growth strategy in the subregion before the disastrous effects of the COVID-19 pandemic. Following the normalization of global travel, tourism-led development will likely return as an important contributor to sustainable growth and development. Beyond recovering from COVID-19 losses, harnessing tourism growth in the longer term will be a key challenge facing the subregion. This article provides an update on tourism arrivals into Samoa and Tonga and explores three potential supply-side challenges that may affect the recovery in both the short and longer terms: the availability of flights, beds, and labor. These factors will also have a significant impact on destination and product development. While some challenges to tourism development will be familiar, others may require significant changes to government policy interventions, particularly for labor supply.

VISITOR ARRIVALS IN A POST-COVID WORLD

As occurred elsewhere in the world, COVID-19-induced border closures all but eliminated visitor arrivals to Samoa and Tonga from early 2020, although a local measles outbreak had impacted arrivals

into Samoa from late 2019. Following the reopening of the borders in August 2022, arrivals have steadily recovered with surging demand among visiting friends and relatives (VFR) in the short term and tourist numbers also showing signs of recovery. From August 2022 to April 2023, 90,915 visitors came to Samoa by air, a 29.8% fall from the same period in FY2019 (ended 30 June for both Samoa and Tonga); and 30,040 visitors arrived by air in Tonga, a 23.2% fall. However, in January–April 2023, Samoan visitor arrivals were only 9.3% lower, and Tongan arrivals were only 8.3% lower than in 2019. Both destinations are on track to reach or exceed their 2019 monthly levels of arrivals by July 2023, a remarkable achievement given the international competition for travelers (Figure 15).

Figure 15: Visitor Arrivals for Samoa and Tonga Relative to 2019

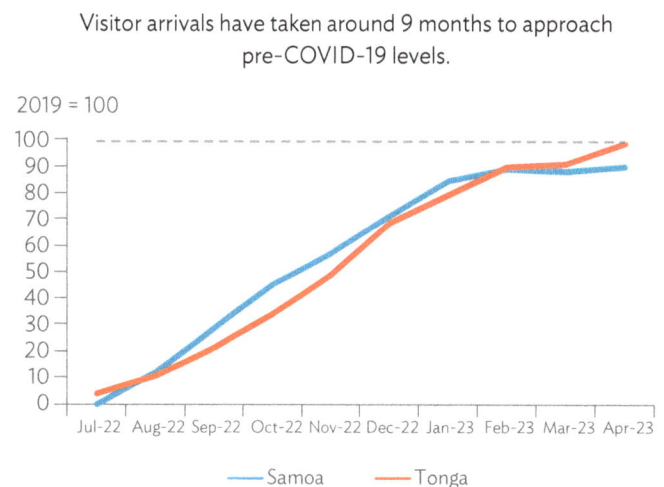

Visitor arrivals have taken around 9 months to approach pre-COVID-19 levels.

2019 = 100

COVID-19 = coronavirus disease.

Note: Data have been smoothed with a 3-month-ended average to reduce volatility in the data series; both series only includes visitor arrivals by air, as arrivals by sea are volatile and often not reported in headline tourism figures.

Sources: Samoa Tourism Authority, Tonga Ministry of Tourism, National Reserve Bank of Tonga.

Following the initial surge of VFR in both countries, VFR has come within the 5-year averages of around 35% of total arrivals into Samoa and approximately 39% in Tonga. Only 33.0% of visitors were classified as tourists in Samoa (down from the 5-year average of 37.8%) and 31.9% in Tonga (down from 39.7%). Visitors not elsewhere classified also made up 17.6% of travelers in Samoa and 20.9% in Tonga, well above the pre-COVID-19 levels, making inferences on movements between categories of visitors challenging. Anecdotally, reporting from government officials suggests that these unclassified travelers are likely to be in the diaspora returning to the islands on foreign passports in large numbers, suggesting VFR figures are stronger than the official data would imply, although this category also includes volunteer and development workers.

AIR ACCESS

Following the almost complete cessation of flights during COVID-19, international airlines faced several challenges when global border restrictions eased, including mounting debt from supporting continued operations during COVID-19; dormant aircraft in storage around the world; and a shortage of pilots and flight crews. While these issues were playing out in other regions of the world, concerns were raised about how smaller destinations in the Pacific could compete for limited aircrews and aircraft availability.

Although service to Samoa from major regional airlines have been recovering toward pre-COVID-19 levels, the loss of routes previously run by Samoa Airways has left a gap compared to pre-COVID-19 capacity, even with Virgin Australia routes returning in March 2023. The total available seats from August 2022 to April 2023 were 162,207, down by 31.0% from the 235,014 seats offered for the same period in FY2019. However, according to the Samoa Tourism Authority, the reduction in seat capacity does not appear to be a binding constraint as around 43,000 of these seats were unused since reopening. Early indications from airlines and forward bookings also suggest that flight capacity will not be a binding constraint in the immediate future. Air New Zealand is increasing the number of 787 Dreamliner flights to five per week (up from three), Virgin Australia has resumed services, and there are limited charter flights from the People's Republic of China.

In Tonga—where the main tourist destination of Vava'u generally requires an additional domestic connection—air routes have been more challenging. According to the Tongan Ministry of Tourism, international seat availability into Tongatapu is yet to be a binding constraint on visitor arrivals, especially with international routes expected to return to pre-COVID-19 levels by September 2023, or earlier. However, due to challenges facing Lulutai Airlines, the domestic connection to Vava'u resumed with only two flights a week run by Fiji Airways. The agreement for these services ceased in June 2023. Lulutai Airlines has taken over the domestic services provided by Fiji Airways, but there have been some transitional disruptions with Lulutai's remaining fleet grounded again in July 2023. However, Fiji Airways has recommenced direct services to Vava'u from Nadi providing additional capacity.

ROOMS AND BEDS

Managing the reopening process for dormant properties has been a global challenge, often requiring significant reinvestment by accommodations owners. This has been made more challenging by an uneven recovery in global traveler demand around the world and across individual accommodators within each market.

In Samoa, COVID-19 added additional financial strain to a sector already weakened by non-performing loans before the pandemic and a measles outbreak in late 2019. Most non-performing loans, by value, were to five large accommodators and originated from a government-backed line of credit during the recovery from Cyclone Evan in 2012. While already well behind on payments before COVID-19, four of the five operators were foreclosed in 2022.[1] Given the dire nature of global tourism, only one of the foreclosed properties has found a buyer that could acquit the pre-existing debts. The properties continue to be partially operated by administrators to maintain cash flow but are yet to bring an estimated one-third of

their rooms back online. Taken together with the baseline challenge of getting existing properties operating after COVID-19, around 10% of all pre-COVID-19 rooms are estimated to still be unavailable as of April 2023. While the Samoan Tourism Authority notes that accommodation capacity is yet to constrain visitor arrivals, there may be challenges in maintaining enough beds to meet traveler demand during the peak season or for the Commonwealth Heads of Government Meeting in 2024.

The challenge is starker in Tonga, which is recovering from the Hunga Tonga-Hunga Ha'apai (HTHH) eruption in 2022 and Tropical Cyclone Harold in 2020. The cyclone damaged around 50 tourism businesses (including 30 accommodators) in the early days of COVID-19.[2] Accommodation businesses were impacted more than any other category. The largest share of damage was borne by three accommodation premises assessed as being "completely destroyed" with a further eight as "severely damaged." Accommodation providers (18%) and room supply (28%) were affected. Before the HTHH event—and 20 months after Tropical Cyclone Harold—more than half of the affected businesses had completed works to recover from cyclone damages. The HTHH event damaged at least 72 tourism businesses (45 accommodators), with 27% of accommodation providers bearing 87% of all private damages and impacting 32% of the total room supply (Figure 16). Some 23 accommodation properties were assessed as "completely destroyed" or "severely damaged" of which half had also faced destruction or severe damage during Tropical Cyclone Harold. Three properties were destroyed twice and are not rebuilt as of this writing. Business owners reported that the insurability of the sites is much more difficult following the twin disasters and may now be unaffordable. One owner reported that while insurance enabled him to begin rebuilding following the cyclone, he was unable to take out builder's risk insurance on the half-finished site before the HTHH event, which wiped out rebuilt structures and washed away construction materials.

Figure 16: Accommodations in Tonga Affected by Disasters in 2020 and 2022

Large losses in accommodation capacity from the 2020 cyclone and 2022 volcanic eruption.

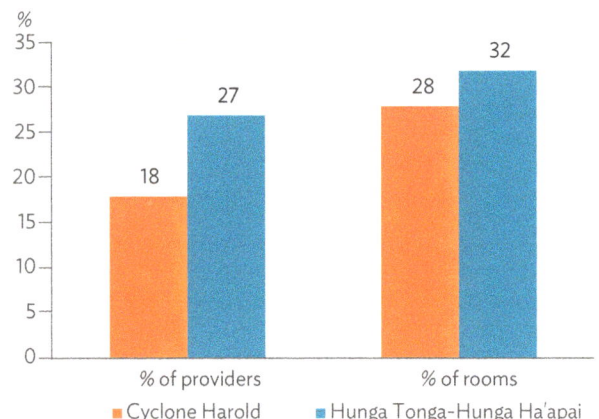

Source: Government of Tonga. 2022. Tonga Tourism Crisis Impacts Assessment Report. Nuku'alofa.

The impact on affected business owners has been immense. Together with COVID-19 impacts, 78% of tourism businesses closed for some or all of 2020–2022, with 50% remaining closed as late as December 2022 (4 months after borders reopened). The total loss of international direct tourism receipts over the border closure period was $183 million, with further anticipated losses of $37 million from August 2022 to December 2023. About 30% of pre-COVID tourism businesses remained closed as of April 2023, with 10% of the total room stock permanently lost. Most of these closures are concentrated among the mid to higher-level accommodation providers in Western Tongatapu, which was most affected by HTHH.

LABOR SUPPLY

The global pandemic had a major impact on labor within the tourism sector. There were large-scale retrenchments during COVID-19 lockdowns, followed by an exodus of labor to other sectors in search of work, better pay, more hours, or better job security amid the uncertainty. The recovery has seen the demand for skilled and semi-skilled workers return at a dramatic pace, straining the ability of labor markets to respond, especially in the Pacific where labor markets are already shallow compared to other international destinations and wages are relatively low compared to Australia or New Zealand (the major destinations for outbound workers).

During the border closures in 2021, almost half (48%) of all tourism workers in Samoa were laid off, with an additional 21% subject to reduced hours.[3] The reopening of borders has enabled travelers to return, but it has also allowed Samoan workers to pursue work opportunities abroad. Combined with workers moving to other service sectors of the economy, total employment in accommodation fell 60.7% during 2019–2022 to just 594 workers. Most other sectors of the economy retained or increased their employment levels. By the third quarter (Q3) of FY2023, employment in the accommodation sector had grown to 842 workers, 44.8% below the pre-COVID-19 level, despite the increase in visitor arrivals. Consultations with private sector peak bodies suggest that vacancies are widespread, with one larger accommodator reporting staff turnover approaching 80% of total workers and months-long challenges in filling vacant positions.

There is no labor force survey information for Tonga, but a mid-2022 industry survey concluded that staffing was a major concern in the industry – at the time of reopening 70% of all the operators raised concerns over the shortage of staff. The National Reserve Bank of Tonga job vacancies survey showed an increase of 106.4% (+450 job vacancies) in total job vacancies advertised through the year to March 2023.[4] More job opportunities were advertised from hotels, restaurants, and business services compared to the previous month, as visitor activity increased but staff were unavailable.

The National Reserve Bank of Tonga indicated regional labor programs and migration for work opportunities as significant challenges to hiring local staff. There are strong incentives for Samoan and Tongan workers to migrate. A study of Tongan migrants showed that seasonal workers typically sent more money

in remittances than they would have earned if living in Tonga, representing an attractive alternative to local employment.[5] When limited travel to New Zealand and Australia became possible in FY2021 and increased further in FY2022, Samoans and Tongans were quick to take advantage.[6] In FY2022, 14.1% of Samoa's and 18.2% of Tonga's male working-age populations were engaged in labor mobility schemes, with Samoa and Tonga being the largest contributors of total workers in the Pacific. Temporary work visas exceeded the size of the public service (the largest single employer in each country) by 49.2% in Samoa and 10.7% in Tonga. In terms of direct impacts, the number of males employed in Samoa fell 3.5% in Q3 FY2023 compared to the pre-COVID-19 peak in Q1 FY2020, while female employment grew 6.2% over the same period. This supports anecdotal reporting from some villages that they are struggling to find enough labor in certain sectors such as agriculture and construction.

CONCLUSION

While total visitor arrivals are nearing their pre-COVID-19 levels, supply-side factors remain a concern for the longer-term development of tourism in Samoa and Tonga. International air access has come back to pre-pandemic levels, although challenges on domestic services in Tonga may disrupt tourism development in the outer islands, including Vava'u. Reinvestment challenges in both countries—albeit for different reasons—may also reduce the ability to expand the tourism industries beyond their previous level of arrivals. This might be a serious concern for Samoa, which is hosting the Commonwealth Heads of Government Meeting in 2024 despite government efforts to reopen and directly invest in Aggie Grey's, the largest accommodator in Apia.[7] For Tonga, the reinvestment challenge is particularly stark for the accommodation providers in western Tongatapu and Ha'apai, who may never rebuild without significant financial aid and insurance solutions. The loss of larger and luxury properties in both countries may impact the ability to invest in marketing abroad, which could have implications for destination marketing overall.

Labor challenges are perhaps the most binding factor on industry expansion if not addressed. Government and local employers will increasingly need to accommodate female workforce participation to meet labor supply needs and look to import workers from abroad, something relatively rare before COVID-19 as there was adequate local labor for most industry needs. The governments of Samoa and Tonga have been expanding access to training to re-skill existing labor, with the Government of Tonga also supporting specialist recruitment from abroad and discussing other options for increasing the availability of short-term workers. These efforts will likely need to increase. However, as the foreign-worker-dependent tourism industry in the Cook Islands discovered during its reopening, the international competition for hospitality workers is fierce—especially from New Zealand and Australia—and facing their own challenges in this area and paying significantly higher wages. This may put pressure on the local wages of hospitality workers to increase, potentially reducing profitability.

Endnotes

[1]   J. Feagaimaalii. 2022. "The degree of indebtedness cannot continue" said Fiame on hotels foreclosed by the DBS. *Radio Polynesia Samoa*. 7 October.

[2]   Government of Tonga. 2022. Tonga Tourism Crisis Impacts Assessment Report. Nuku'alofa.

[3]   Pacific Private Sector Development Initiative. 2021. *Pacific Tourism Sector Snapshot: Samoa*. Sydney.

[4]   National Reserve Bank of Tonga. 2023. Monthly Economic Update (April 2023).

[5]   R. Edwards; M. Dornan; D. Doan; and T. Nguyen. 2022. Three questions on Tongan remittances. *DevPolicy*. Canberra.

[6]   For a closer examination of trends in remittances and migration in Samoa and Tonga, please refer to the December 2022 issue of the Pacific Economic Monitor.

[7]   *Samoa Observer/Pacnews*. 2023. Samoa Government takes over $30 million Aggie Greys hotel shares. 22 June.

Logging off: Exploring new growth engines for Solomon Islands

Lead authors: Prince Cruz and Dalcy Tozaka

Since the 1990s, forestry and logging have dominated the economy of Solomon Islands, both in terms of exports and overall government revenue. However, in 2022 log output fell for the fourth consecutive year. Output at 1.6 million cubic meters (m³) in 2022 was 20.8% lower than the previous year, the sharpest annual decline ever recorded. It was also around half of the peak level of 3 million m³ in 2016 (Figure 17). Exports of log and timber similarly declined from a peak of $384 million in 2018 to $176 million in 2022. Forestry and logging output has been over maximum sustainable yield for many years. While COVID-19-induced lockdowns played a role in the decline, it is also part of a longer-term shift toward more sustainable logging output.

Logs and timber accounted for an average of 70.0% of exports from 2015 to 2020, valued at around $317 million each year (21.3% of GDP). With the decline during the pandemic, the share of logs and timber to total exports declined to 46.8% in 2022. The fall in log exports contributed to a rising trade deficit which reached $206 million (equivalent to 13.6% of GDP) in 2022 (Figure 18). Logging provides crucial foreign currency that is needed for key imports including food, fuel, basic manufactured goods, and machinery and transport equipment.

Figure 18: Solomon Islands Trade Balance and Components

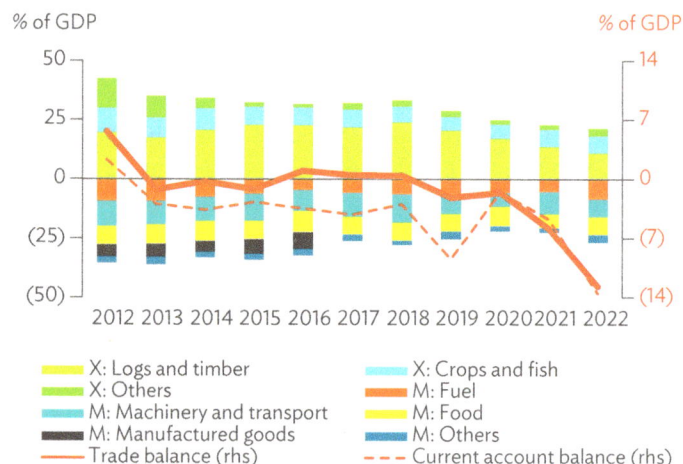

GDP = gross domestic product, M = import, rhs = right-hand scale, X = export.
Sources: Central Bank of Solomon Islands. 2023. *Quarterly Review December 2022*. Honiara; ADB estimates.

In 2022, exports of crops (palm oil and kernels, cocoa, copra, and coconut oil) accounted for 18.1% of total exports, while exports of fish accounted for 15.7% of total exports. This was despite an increase in the total value of fish exports from an annual average of $48 million in 2015–2020 to $56 million in 2021–2022 (Figure 19). Other exports include coffee, kava, vanilla, and spices.

Figure 17: Solomon Islands Log Output and Exports

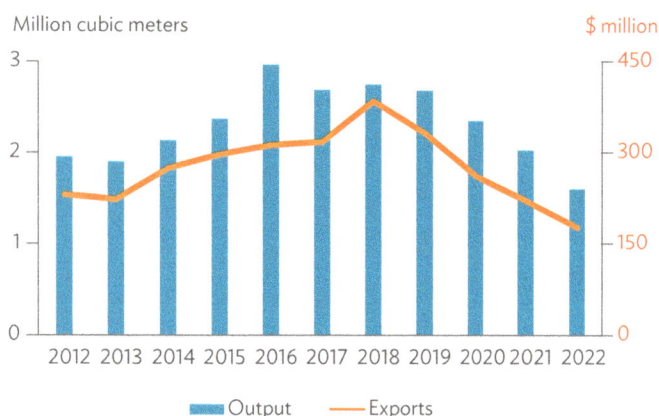

Sources: Central Bank of Solomon Islands. 2023. *Quarterly Review December 2022*. Honiara; ADB estimates.

Figure 19: Solomon Islands Exports of Fish and Crops

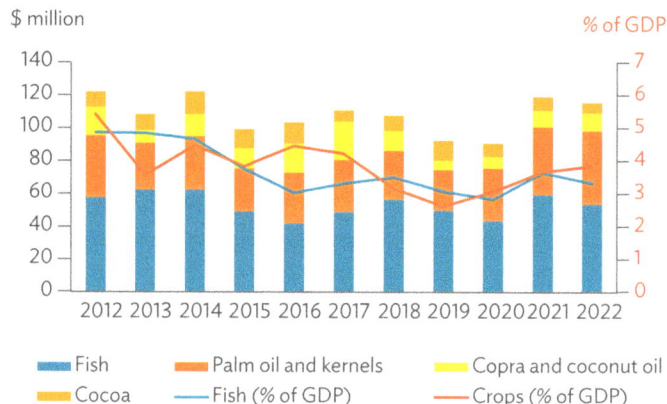

GDP = gross domestic product.
Sources: Central Bank of Solomon Islands. 2023. *Quarterly Review December 2022*. Honiara; ADB estimates.

With log output and exports expected to continue declining, Solomon Islands requires new drivers of growth. The sectors widely considered to have strong potential are fishing, crop production and livestock, and tourism. In 2022, the value of crops and fish exports was less than 4% of GDP, while tourism contributed around 2%, down from an average of 7% in 2016–2019 (Figure 20). From 2012 to 2022, exports of logs were larger than the sum of tourism receipts and exports of fish and crops. This article explores the challenges and opportunities for these industries and current government initiatives to foster their growth.

Figure 20: Solomon Islands Tourism Arrivals and Receipts

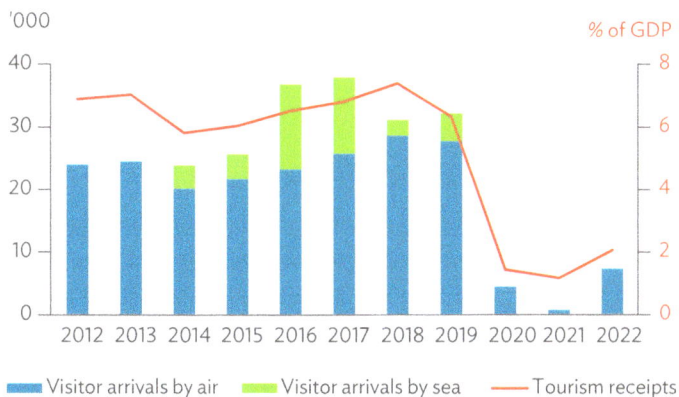

GDP = gross domestic product.
Sources: Central Bank of Solomon Islands. 2023. *Quarterly Review December 2022*. Honiara; ADB estimates.

Project which was launched in 2022 with the support of the World Bank. Fully aligned with ASGIP, the SIART Project aims to support 85,000 Solomon Islanders with training, farming and livestock support services, and infrastructure to help communities increase agricultural productivity.[4] In anticipation of increased demand for food for the 2023 Pacific Games, the Ministry of Agriculture and Livestock is also supporting farmers and promoting supply chain improvements to increase production.

Figure 21: Solomon Islands Household Engagement in Agriculture

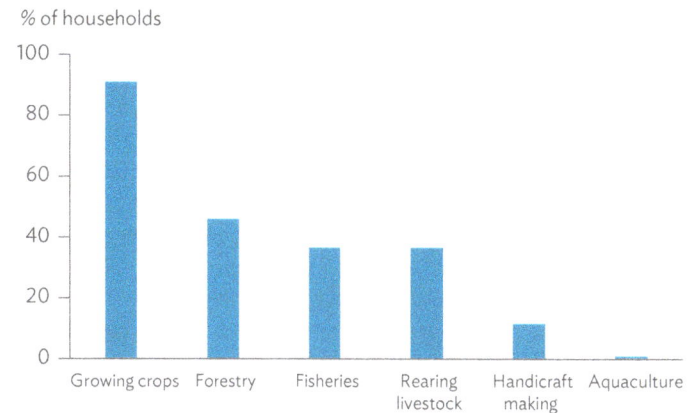

Note: Figures recalculated from the percent of agricultural households in the report to the percent of all households. The question allowed multiple answers.
Source: Government of Solomon Islands. 2019. *Report on National Agricultural Survey 2017*. Honiara.

CROP PRODUCTION AND LIVESTOCK

Although more than 90% of households engage in agricultural crop production and 36% of households raise livestock such as pigs and chickens, this is mainly for home consumption (Figure 21).[1] The 2017 Agricultural Census noted that the most lucrative crops were coconut, betelnut, cocoa, cassava, and kumara, but "each yielded only slightly more than half of the expected attainable yield in sales. In large part this reflects the fact that much of the harvested crop remained unsold."[2] The agriculture sector is beset with challenges including limited access to markets and transportation, insufficient financing and technical expertise, and geographic and land-ownership constraints.

To address these challenges, the government adopted the Agriculture Sector Growth and Investment Plan (ASGIP) 2021–2030 to strengthen, modernize, and commercialize the sector. It provides a guide for public and private sectors, promoting interventions to support economic growth, food security, and employment.

Under ASGIP, in February 2023 the Ministry of Agriculture and Livestock launched the New Day Strategy, which encourages multiple generations to engage in agricultural activities beyond the subsistence level, particularly youth.[3] The New Day Strategy is part of the Solomon Islands Agriculture and Rural Transformation (SIART)

To boost the export of crops as targeted in ASGIP, in 2021 the government revitalized the Commodity Exporting Marketing Authority (CEMA). Established in 1984, CEMA is tasked to purchase, sell, and export commodities and to establish refineries for downstream processing of crops for export and domestic use. To increase the production of goods for export markets, CEMA established various centers in provincial areas. For example, in December 2021 a refinery and buying center was established in Noro, Western Province, and in May 2022, another buying center was opened at Pakera in Makira-Ulawa Province. These buying centers and refineries purchase cocoa and copra, with plans to extend into other agricultural products. Buying centers in five other provincial sites and one in Honiara are planned. In June 2022, the government renamed CEMA into Solomon Commodities with the brand "Solomon Is. Organic."[5]

FISHING AND MARINE RESOURCES

Like crop production, the fisheries sector has tremendous potential. While fishing license revenues contribute significantly to nontax revenue, the government is focused on maximizing untapped revenues from domestic fishing activities.[6] The Ministry of Fisheries and Marine Resources has estimated that the country has the potential to harvest as much as 90,000 metric tons of tuna annually. This compares with an annual (as of 2023) production of between

25,000 and 30,000 metric tons from the country's sole tuna processing operation in Noro, Western Province.[7] While 36% of households engage in fisheries, only 3% do so mainly for sale while 21% engage in fishing mainly for consumption and occasional sale Less than 1% of households engage in aquaculture (Figure 21).

To ensure the conservation, management, and sustainable development of marine resources, the Ministry of Fisheries and Marine Resources is implementing the Solomon Islands National Fisheries Policy 2019–2029, with three main policy areas: (i) inshore and inland fisheries, (ii) offshore fisheries, and (iii) aquaculture.[8] For offshore fisheries, the focus is on processing and exporting tuna. To increase processing capability, a tuna processing plant is planned for Bina Harbour in Malaita Province. It is expected to create more than 5,500 new jobs and generate foreign direct investment of $40 million through public–private partnerships.[9] Onshore processing of this valuable resource could be a strong source of revenue.

For freshwater fisheries and aquaculture, the government is focusing on the cultivation of Nile tilapia (a type of fish), which is expected to boost incomes while providing a relatively cheap source of protein. Other aquaculture activities include farming pearl oysters, giant clams, and seaweed, which are supported by different private sector partners.

In recognition of the important role communities play in resource management, the government has also developed the Community Based Coastal and Marine Resource Management Strategy 2021–2025. The strategy outlines activities to scale up support for community-based resource management (CBRM) across the country and increase the capacity and involvement of provincial authorities. The strategy targets 25% of coastal, watershed, and inshore areas to be under improved management through CBRM by 2025. Improved CBRM will help improve industry sustainability.

TOURISM

Compared to nearby Fiji and Vanuatu, the tourism sector is underdeveloped in Solomon Islands. The 7,327 visitor arrivals in 2022 were less than 25% of arrivals in 2019 when 27,730 visitors arrived by air and 4,321 by sea.[10] Solomon Islands' tourism potential is largely untapped. The Pacific Private Sector Development Initiative (2021) has identified a number of challenges including:[11]

(i)   The difficulty of domestic travel that limits visitation to outer islands;
(ii)   Unreliable and costly energy supply;
(iii) Poor waste management and sanitation services;
(iv)   A weak business environment that limits foreign investment;
(v)   Lack of access to finance for tourism operators;
(vi)   Limited tourism skills and insufficient training capacities; and
(vii) Complex landownership systems.

To address the challenges in accessing suitable land for tourism developments, the International Finance Corporation developed a comprehensive tourism investor guide for Solomon Islands, which highlights investment-ready land suitable for tourism development.[12]

The government Solomon Islands Tourism Recovery Plan 2021–2030 is the country's interim sector strategy and recovery plan, intended to: (i) return the industry to its 2019 position, and (ii) expand with a target of 100,000 arrivals per year by 2035. It details five points for recovery: restoration, extra care, future, reset, and measurement.

In addition to general sector recovery, there is increasing focus on the potential of expanding the expedition cruise ship market. The smaller cruise ships (70 to 150 passengers) can dock at a wide range of ports around the country. Appealing to bird watchers, mountaineers, explorers, and nature enthusiasts, passengers of expedition cruise ships stay for several days, with a spending profile like visitors by air. To attract more cruise expeditions, more could be done in terms of preparing and training local communities to accept more visitors and upgrading infrastructure and other port facilities.

CONCLUSION

With log output expected to continue declining and the population rapidly expanding, the challenges faced by Solomon Islands are daunting. There is an immediate need to develop alternative sources of growth that are more inclusive and economically and environmentally sustainable. Aside from the specific concerns of each industry discussed, general concerns such as the high cost of doing business and the costly but unreliable supply of utilities (including electricity, telecommunications, and water and sanitation) must be addressed. Addressing the infrastructure gap for improved connectivity is crucial for these growth drivers.

Given the limited financial resources in the country, improving the business environment to encourage more public–private partnerships and foreign direct investments must also be prioritized. Projects that encourage engagement in commercial agriculture, support community-based resource management, strengthen the capacity of provincial agriculture officers to monitor and support local farmers, and expand integrated and intersectoral developments (such as agritourism) are expected to boost broad-based growth.

Endnotes

[1] For instance, only 40% of the 54 million kilograms of crops harvested in the year prior to the 2017 Agricultural Census were sold. Among the major crops, only cocoa has more households raising it mainly for sale (14% of households) than home consumption (less than 1%). Government of Solomon Islands. 2019. *Report on National Agricultural Survey 2017.* Honiara.

[2] Government of Solomon Islands. 2019. *Report on National Agricultural Survey 2017.* Honiara.

[3] Government of Solomon Islands. 2023. Solomon Islands Agriculture and Rural Transformation Project Steering Committee meeting discussed new MAL direction. Honiara (7 March).

[4] World Bank. 2022. Boost for Agricultural Production and Cash Crops in Solomon Islands. Press release. Washington, D.C. (17 March).

5   Government of Solomon Islands. 2022. Farmers celebrate CEMA "Renaming and Branding." Honiara (2 June).
6   As a member of the Parties to the Nauru Agreement (PNA), Solomon Islands earns around SI$300 million annually from fishing license revenues. This forms the bulk of nontax revenues, which account for around 10% of total revenues and grants. Although fishing license revenues are a strong revenue earner, they are significantly more substantial for other PNA members located closer to the equator, where potential catch is greater.
7   Solomon Times. 2023. Solomon Islands Marks World Tuna Day 2023. 3 May.
8   Government of Solomon Islands, Ministry of Fisheries and Marine Resources. 2019. Solomon Islands National Fisheries Policy 2019–2029. Honiara.
9   International Finance Corporation. 2022. Transformative Project to Deliver Thousands of Jobs and Economic Security for Solomon Islands. Honiara (3 May).
10 Arrivals to Solomon Islands in 2019 were significantly lower compared to 120,628 to Vanuatu and 894,389 to Fiji. Pacific Tourism Organization. 2022. Quarter 4, 2020 Visitor Arrivals Snapshot. Suva.
11 Pacific Private Sector Development Initiative (PSDI). 2021. Solomon Islands: Pacific Tourism Snapshot. Sydney (November).
12 International Finance Corporation. 2021. Solomon Islands Tourism Industry Guides for Investors and Government. Washington, DC.

Vanuatu: Disasters and resilience during the pandemic

Lead authors: Prince Cruz and Katherine Passmore

In the first week of March 2023, Vanuatu was hit by two category 4 tropical cyclones and earthquakes that affected more than 80% of the population. These came as the country was still recovering from the effects of category 5 tropical cyclone Pam in 2015 and tropical cyclone Harold in 2020, and several other disasters triggered by natural hazards including volcanic eruptions, drought, and insect infestation. The impact of these events was exacerbated by COVID-19. This article tracks the economic cost of these disasters and the responses by the government and development partners.

Vanuatu is one of the economies at the most risk of disaster triggered by natural hazards in the world (Box 1). From 1980 to 2020, Vanuatu experienced more than 50 disasters triggered by natural hazards, affecting up to 90% of the population, particularly due to the impact of tropical cyclones (Figure 22).

The twin cyclones Judy and Kevin in March 2023 caused substantial damage. According to initial government estimates, the March 2023 tropical cyclones affected approximately 251,000 people i.e., 80% of the population.[1] The total impact of loss and damage has been estimated at $433 million, with the greatest loss being in the agriculture sector (upon which many livelihoods depend), and the greatest damage in the housing sector. More

than 6,000 houses were destroyed, and more than double that were damaged. Tourism—which typically accounts for upward of 20% of GDP—also experienced a shock because of the cyclones, despite Vanuatu having only reopened its borders in July 2022 from COVID-19 closures.[2] The government has revised its 2023 GDP growth forecast from 3.6% to 3.0%. Inflation is expected to rise, particularly as the loss in agricultural production will reduce the domestic food supply.[3] This is likely to be compounded by the expected El Niño season, which may also affect domestic crop production.

Figure 22: Population Affected by Disasters in Vanuatu

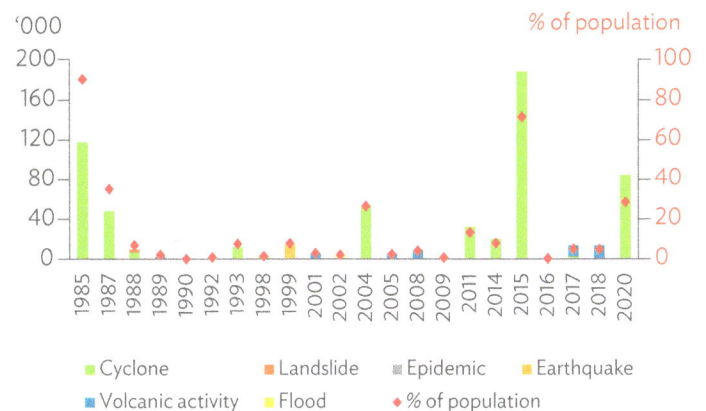

Source: World Bank. Climate Change Knowledge Portal; ADB estimates.

The social and economic impact of such disasters is immense. Modeling by the Pacific Catastrophe Risk Assessment Financing Initiative estimates that on a long-term average, Vanuatu is expected to incur $48 million annually in losses because of earthquakes and cyclones. The modeling suggests that in a 50-year time frame, Vanuatu has a 50% chance of a disaster resulting in a loss greater than $330 million with fatalities exceeding 725 people, and a 10% chance of a disaster resulting in a loss greater than $540 million with fatalities exceeding 2,150 people.[4] Government estimates of damage, loss, and recovery requirements from the more recent disasters triggered by natural hazards are sizable relative to GDP (Table 1). The frequency and severity of these disasters mean that recovery efforts from one event may still be ongoing at the time of the next disaster. From an economic perspective, such events dampen growth prospects, create inflationary pressures, and affect monetary, fiscal, and balance of payment outlooks.

In addition to tropical cyclones, Vanuatu is exposed to a variety of other disasters triggered by natural hazards that compound damaging effects on livelihoods and the economy, slow down recovery efforts, and add strain to limited recovery resources. Recent events include eruptions of active volcanoes and a coconut rhinoceros beetle (CRB) outbreak. The eruption of the Ambae volcano in 2017 and 2018 resulted in evacuation and permanent resettlement of 11,000 residents, while the emergence of the CRB

Table 1: Magnitude and Impact of a Sample of Tropical Cyclones in Vanuatu, 2015–2023

Year	Disaster	Impact: damage and loss ($ million)	Other impacts (# of HHs affected, fatalities)	Recovery estimate ($ million)
2015	Tropical Cyclone Pam (category 5)	449 (64% of GDP)	40,000 HH affected/ 80% population 11 fatalities	316
2020	Tropical Cyclone Harold (category 5)	508[a] (50% of GDP)	26,359 HH affected/ 43% population 3 fatalities	358
2023	Tropical Cyclones Judy and Kevin (category 4)	433 (40% of GDP)	43,623 HH affected/ 80% population No fatalities reported	773

GDP = gross domestic product; HH = households.

[a] Estimate based on adjusted figures.

Sources: ADB. Vanuatu: Tropical Cyclone Judy and Tropical Cyclone Kevin Emergency Response Project; Government of Vanuatu, Department of Strategic Policy, Planning and Aid Coordination. 2020. *Post-Disaster Needs Assessment: TC Harold and COVID-19*. Port Vila; Government of Vanuatu, Department of Strategic Policy, Planning and Aid Coordination. 2023. *Post Disaster Needs Assessment: Vanuatu Tropical Cyclones Judy and Kevin*. Port Vila; Government of Vanuatu, Prime Minister's Office. 2015. *Vanuatu Post-Disaster Needs Assessment: Tropical Cyclone Pam*. Port Vila.

in 2019 poses significant risk to the country's coconut industry and associated livelihoods.[5] In 2019, the government declared a state of emergency to enable control of CRB infected areas, but post-cyclone conditions are expected to lead to further outbreaks.[6] While Vanuatu has taken measures to climate-proof infrastructure and establish an emergency fund for immediate disaster response, revenue from the Honorary Citizenship Program[7]—which accounted for an average of 31% of revenue during 2019–2021—is on the decline.[8] To counterbalance this decline, the government will need to continue efforts to mobilize domestic revenue and access concessional financing.

Government initiatives and financing are supported by a range of development partners, including (i) adaptation and mitigation projects, (ii) emergency support in the aftermath of disasters, including contingent disaster financing, (iii) preparation of post-disaster needs assessments, and (iv) funding and implementation support for recovery efforts. The government has expressed a preference for donor funding to be provided as direct budget support, but it is willing to accept support through other modalities.[9] To manage debt sustainability, the government has restricted external borrowing to concessional terms only.[10] Regardless of modality, support from development partners is essential to meet financing needs and relieve fiscal pressure.[11] The government will be unable to absorb the cost of repeated disasters triggered by natural hazards without donor support.

The government continues to refine its institutional frameworks for disaster preparedness, risk reduction, and recovery. This includes the adoption of the Vanuatu Climate Change and Disaster Risk Reduction Policy 2016–2030, the development of the National Disaster Recovery Framework 2021, and the Disaster Risk Management Act 2019. These measures are important to ensure

strategic and well-coordinated efforts, from both government and development partners. The Climate Change and Disaster Risk Reduction Policy aims to ensure sufficient resources are available for risk reduction activities, build the capability to manage these resources and enhance access to international funding. As more international funding becomes available, strong governance and financial management mechanisms will be essential.

The severity of hydrometeorological events is expected to increase due to climate change.[12] Modeling suggests that due to warmer sea surface temperatures, more intense tropical cyclones are likely.[13] One of the government's guiding principles in its Recovery Strategy 2020–2023 is to "build back better," which focuses on the resilience of infrastructure, community, the environment, and the economy. While the recovery strategy for the March 2023 cyclones is under development, the climate outlook reaffirms the criticality of dedicated government resources in this area.

CONCLUSION

Vanuatu is frequently subject to extreme disasters triggered by natural hazards with major social and economic impacts. Disaster response and recovery require significant fiscal resources, while economic recovery can take years. With significant financing implications, the government should continue to expand sources of domestic revenue, access international financial support, and carefully prioritize available funding. Support from development partners will help Vanuatu meet its financing needs, while the continued pursuit of concessional financing will support debt sustainability and help to build and preserve fiscal reserves to better absorb disaster and climate-related shocks.

Box 1: Is Vanuatu the most at-risk country in the world?

From 2011 to 2021, Vanuatu ranked number one globally in the WorldRiskIndex as the most at-risk country in terms of exposure and vulnerability (or susceptibility) to disasters. In the 2022 WorldRiskIndex, Vanuatu's rank lowered significantly to 49. This significant adjustment in rank was due to a revised ranking methodology, including adjustments for population wherein "both absolute and percentage figures of the population at risk are included in the calculation. This avoids a distortion due to population size." The methodology was also adjusted to include additional indicators resulting in more ADB Pacific developing member countries (DMCs) receiving a rank (out of 192 countries, Nauru ranked 180, Palau 173, Tuvalu 162, and the Marshall Islands 139).

In the 2022 WorldRiskIndex, the Vanuatu score for "exposure" moved down to the second highest risk quintile, while its "vulnerability" and "susceptibility" are only considered as "medium" (in the middle quintile). According to the revised methodology, among Pacific DMCs, Papua New Guinea and Solomon Islands are considered more at risk than Vanuatu (Figure B1).

Despite the change in its ranking, Vanuatu remains one of the most at-risk countries. Its geographic location in the South Pacific tropical cyclone basin and the Pacific Ring of Fire remains unchanged and its institutional capacity to respond to disasters is still limited (Figure B2). More can be done in terms of strengthening its coping and adaptive capacities.

Figure B1: WorldRiskIndex Rankings of ADB Pacific Developing Member Countries 2020–2022

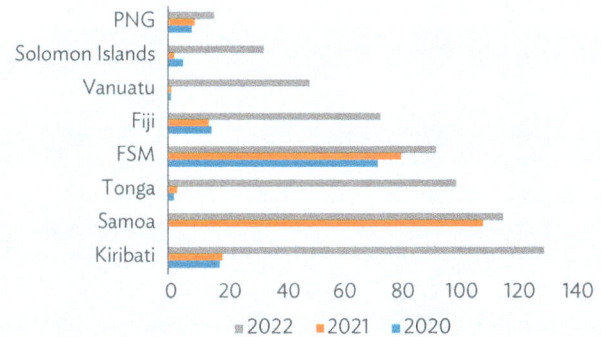

ADB = Asian Development Bank, FSM = Federated States of Micronesia, PNG = Papua New Guinea

Note: Lower rank denotes higher risk. Comparison out of 192 economies in 2022 and 181 in 2021 and 2020.

Source: *WorldRiskReport* 2020, 2021, 2022 (accessed 15 June 2023).

Figure B2: Vanuatu WorldRiskIndex Score 2020–2022

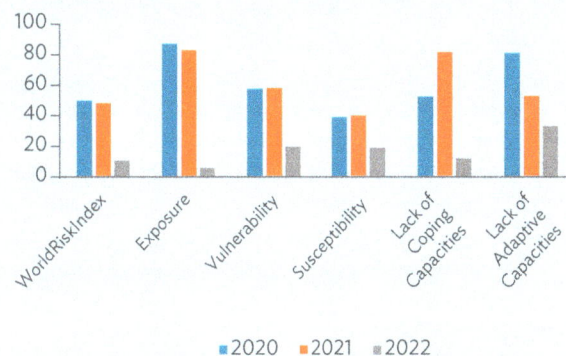

Source: *WorldRiskReport* 2020, 2021, 2022 (accessed 15 June 2023).

Endnotes

1 Government of Vanuatu, Department of Strategic Policy, Planning and Aid Coordination. 2023. *Post Disaster Needs Assessment: Vanuatu Tropical Cyclones Judy and Kevin*. Port Vila.
2 Pacific Private Sector Development Initiative. 2021. *Vanuatu Pacific Tourism Sector Snapshot*. Sydney.
3 Government of Vanuatu, Department of Strategic Policy, Planning and Aid Coordination. 2023. *Post Disaster Needs Assessment: Vanuatu Tropical Cyclones Judy and Kevin*. Port Vila.
4 Pacific Catastrophe Risk Assessment and Financing Initiative. 2011. *Country Risk Profile: Vanuatu*.
5 E.A. Roy. 2018. Island of no return: Vanuatu evacuates entire population of volcanic Ambae. *The Guardian*. 19 April.
6 Radio New Zealand. 2023. Post-cyclone rhinoceros beetle outbreak concerns in Vanuatu. 11 April.
7 The Honorary Citizenship program provides Vanuatu citizenship and a passport in exchange for investment.

8 ADB. 2023. *Asian Development Outlook*. Manila.
9 Government of Vanuatu, Disaster Recovery Coordination Unit. 2020. *Vanuatu Recovery Strategy 2020–2023*. Port Vila.
10 International Monetary Fund (IMF). 2023. *Vanuatu: Staff Report for the 2023 Article IV Consultation*. IMF Country Report No. 23/115. Washington, DC.
11 ADB has provided only grant financing to Vanuatu since 2020.
12 World Bank Group. 2021. *Dealing with disasters: Analyzing Vanuatu's economy and public finances through the lens of disaster resilience*. Washington, DC.
13 World Bank Group. 2021. *Dealing with disasters: Analyzing Vanuatu's economy and public finances through the lens of disaster resilience*. Washington, DC.

POLICY BRIEFS

Women's economic empowerment in the Pacific

This policy brief highlights the key findings and recommendations from the publication *Women's Economic Empowerment in the Pacific Region*, a comprehensive analysis of research and data on women's economic empowerment in Pacific island countries. The analysis focuses on women's entrepreneurship and micro, small, and medium-sized enterprises owned by women. Drawing on over 200 published papers and studies and 11 quantitative datasets, it looks at what fosters and what hinders women's economic empowerment in the Pacific. It considers business ownership, formalization, and expansion; the association between women's economic empowerment and violence against women and girls (VAWG); and the effects of the coronavirus disease (COVID-19) pandemic.

Micro, small, and medium-sized enterprises play a central role in economic development in the Pacific island countries and offer pathways to women's leadership and economic empowerment. This summary brief explores the state of knowledge on women's economic empowerment in the Pacific island countries, with a focus on women entrepreneurs and women-owned micro, small, and medium-sized enterprises (MSMEs).

Promoting women's economic empowerment is a strategic operational priority of the Asian Development Bank (ADB), governments, and civil society in Pacific developing member countries. ADB's Strategy 2030 aims to support quality job generation and higher value-added entrepreneurship opportunities for women as a way of narrowing gender gaps in the world of work.

STATUS AND TRENDS IN WOMEN'S ECONOMIC EMPOWERMENT

Women have lower labor force participation rates and are more likely to work in the informal economy. Women's labor force participation ranged from 34% in Samoa to 84% in Solomon Islands in 2019. The employment rate for women is 30 percentage points lower for Tuvalu and more than 20 percentage points lower in the Marshall Islands and Samoa, compared with men (ILO 2020). Prior to the COVID-19 pandemic, female labor force participation rates in the Pacific showed a slight increase from 51% in 1999 to 55% in 2019. In the Pacific, it is mainly women who work in the informal economy, often in low productivity jobs with limited capital and skills accumulation potential. Low levels of labor force participation and concentration in the informal economy limit women's access to social protection—including in older age—reinforcing vulnerability and poverty.

There is occupational segregation in the Pacific, and women have weaker agency than men. Women are overrepresented in undervalued occupations in the services sector: tourism, the garment industry, food processing, health, and social work. While women's representation in business leadership is favorable compared with global averages, on average, women have far less representation on boards and in CEO positions.

Women carry the burden of unpaid care and domestic work, and lack of access to affordable and quality childcare is a key challenge for working parents, particularly women.

- Women in Fiji spend three times as much time on unpaid domestic work and care work than men (Fiji Bureau of Statistics 2016).
- A survey by the International Finance Corporation (IFC) of more than 2,700 employees in Fiji found that only 8% of parents with pre-school-age children use a childcare service (IFC 2019a).

Pacific women—especially those in remote areas—have lower levels of access to digital technology than men despite strong evidence of its potential to improve business outcomes. Digital technology allows women to reach new markets, reduce travel costs, order supplies, and provide records of savings and transactions, which improves their ability to secure loans. The main barriers to women's access to digital technologies are low awareness of the potential benefits of such technologies, limited affordability of services, men's coercive control over their partner's access to information, and women's perception that access would make their husbands suspicious.

Pacific women are more likely to experience the negative effects of climate change and disasters as they are less likely to have access to the resources and information they would need to adapt and respond (ILO 2017). Climate change and disasters triggered by natural hazards disproportionately affect industries such as agriculture, fisheries, and tourism where women work and in which women-owned businesses are concentrated (ADB 2019).

While most Pacific island countries have laws and policies that promote gender equality and aim to give women equal economic opportunities, there are weaknesses in existing legislation and uneven enforcement. According to Women, Business and the Law, since 2008, most Pacific island countries have introduced domestic violence legislation. Most countries in the subregion have ratified the Convention on the Elimination of All Forms of Discrimination against Women (World Bank 2021). However, customary law often precludes women from inheriting and owning land. Across all Pacific island countries, laws mandating equal remuneration for work of equal value and legislation on sexual harassment in the workplace are the least commonly enacted.

OWNERSHIP, FORMALIZATION, AND EXPANSION OF BUSINESS

Women's entrepreneurship is common in the Pacific, especially in family businesses. However, women-owned MSMEs are smaller and more likely to be in the informal economy (Figure 1). Women-owned businesses in the Pacific are typically concentrated in agriculture, retail, restaurants, hospitality and tourism, and handicrafts. There is some evidence that women in the Pacific are increasingly becoming entrepreneurs (FAO 2019, UNESCAP 2020). Women-owned businesses tend to employ more women than large (mostly male-owned) firms (ADB 2019).

Both supply-side and demand-side initiatives have increased women's access to finance. Access to finance can result in greater involvement of women in decisions about household spending, establishment and growth of women-owned businesses, and increased savings.

Supply-side initiatives include banks expanding access to credit via a wider range of "lending products," greater flexibility in eligibility criteria, lower rates of interest, and more flexible repayment schemes. Various Pacific island countries have progressed toward a secure transaction framework, which has encouraged women to take out loans. Demand-side initiatives include business and financial literacy training, mentoring, and microfinance support (ADB 2019).

Many Pacific island countries have a weak enabling environment for promoting women's business and entrepreneurship, but digital processes are the most widely cited positive change (Figure 2). For example, in Tonga, one can apply for a business license online, which is quicker and avoids transport costs and fees that are

Figure 1. Percentage of Women-Owned Micro, Small, and Medium-Sized Enterprises, By Sector

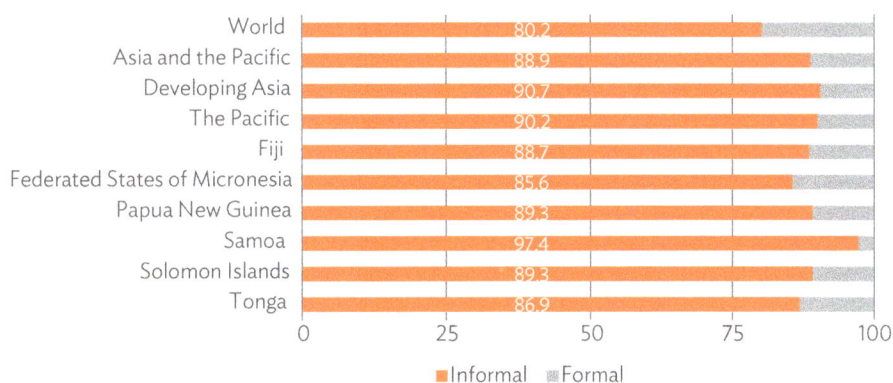

	Informal
World	80.2
Asia and the Pacific	88.9
Developing Asia	90.7
The Pacific	90.2
Fiji	88.7
Federated States of Micronesia	85.6
Papua New Guinea	89.3
Samoa	97.4
Solomon Islands	89.3
Tonga	86.9

■ Informal   ▨ Formal

Note: Statistics do not include the Marshall Islands; Myanmar: Nauru; Palau; Taipei,China; Tuvalu; and Vanuatu.

Source: ADB. 2019. *Leveraging Trade for Women's Economic Empowerment in the Pacific*. Manila.

Figure 2: Main Barriers to the Expansion and Formalization of Women-Owned Businesses in the Pacific

Social norms

Gender stereotypes can limit women's business aspirations, opportunities, and access to support. Unpaid work burdens also limit the expansion and formalization of women-owned businesses.

Access to commercial finance

Women's limited ownership of private land restricts the use of land as a collateral for commercial finance.

Business literacy, skills, and access to information

There is limited access to skills development programs and a lack of information on business regulations and procedures. Market analyses and business plans are often not conducted.

Voice and accountability

Women in business are less likely to be consulted for their views, and justice systems are not set up to be accessible for women in resolving commercial disputes.

Source: ADB. 2023. *Women's Economic Empowerment in the Pacific Region: A Comprehensive Analysis of Existing Research and Data*. Manila.

particularly burdensome for time-poor women. However, women in the Pacific are less likely than men to have access to a computer or a smartphone and are less likely to have the digital literacy skills to use online platforms. Gender-responsive procurement has potential although progress is hampered by weak policy and legislative frameworks.

There are a wide variety of business networks in the Pacific, but due to capacity constraints and funding gaps, their remit is mainly around building access to and ownership of assets, capabilities, and opportunities for women. There is little evidence of seeking transformational changes that address unequal power relations and systemic institutional, legal, and societal barriers for women.

ASSOCIATION BETWEEN WOMEN'S ECONOMIC EMPOWERMENT AND VIOLENCE AGAINST WOMEN AND GIRLS

Violence against women and girls—including economic abuse— is prevalent in the Pacific. Almost 27% of ever-partnered women in the Marshall Islands reported that their partners either took their earnings or refused to give them money (ADB 2019).

Violence has high costs for businesses (Figure 3). An IFC survey of 1,200 employees in Solomon Islands found that time at work lost due to violence at home totals 2 working weeks per year per employee surveyed (IFC 2019b).

Figure 3: Impact of Partner Violence on Women's Paid Work

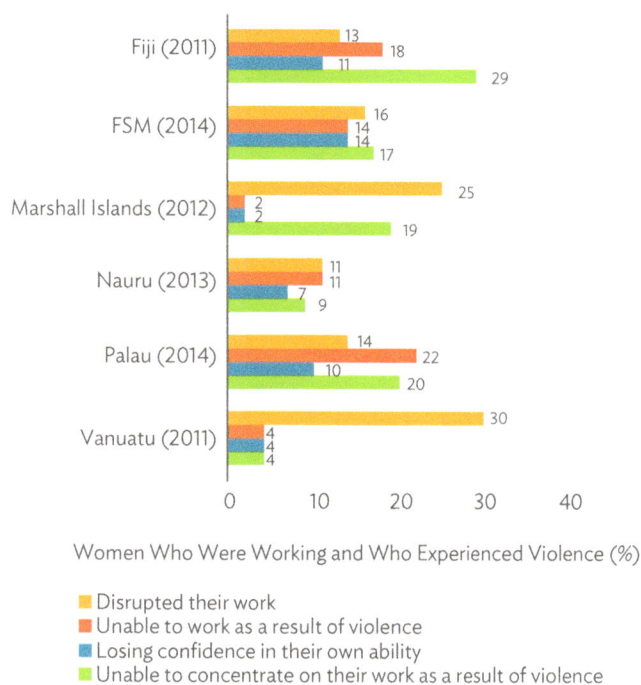

Women Who Were Working and Who Experienced Violence (%)

- Disrupted their work
- Unable to work as a result of violence
- Losing confidence in their own ability
- Unable to concentrate on their work as a result of violence

FSM = Federated States of Micronesia.
Sources: Pacific Data Hub; Vanuatu Women's Centre. 2011. *Vanuatu National Survey on Women's Lives and Family Relationships*. Port Vila.

There is mixed evidence about the correlation between women's increasing incomes and intimate partner violence.

- A survey of 3,538 households in Fiji found that women's economic empowerment can be a key pathway to support women to leave a violent relationship (Fiji Women's Crisis Centre 2013). Increased income can also lessen stress and tension in the household.
- In Vanuatu, women who have their own source of income are around 1.5 times more likely to experience physical and sexual violence than those who do not (ADB 2019).

Civil society, businesses, and women's business networks have all played a key role in increasing awareness of and support to address violence against women and girls in the Pacific.

For instance:

- The Fiji Women's Rights Movement initiated the "Not OK: Stop Sexual Harassment" campaign which was a part of a successful lobby to ratify the International Labour Organization (ILO) Convention 190, an international treaty on violence and harassment at work.
- The Meri Seif (Women Safe) bus scheme in Papua New Guinea (PNG) has provided almost 150,000 women and girls a safe journey to their job, school, or the market (Pacific Women 2021).

Early signs show that interventions partnering with the private sector are effective in addressing violence against women workers. Fifteen large companies in Solomon Islands have committed to introducing policies for respectful workplaces under the Waka Mere project (Pacific Women 2021). An IFC survey found much lower levels of acceptance of domestic and sexual violence among Waka Mere employees compared to the general population, which could indicate that workplace responses can improve attitudes toward violence (IFC 2019b).

EFFECTS OF THE COVID-19 PANDEMIC

Women entrepreneurs, women-owned MSMEs, and women workers have been particularly negatively affected by the COVID-19 pandemic. Although initially Pacific island countries had relatively few cases of COVID-19, government responses through border closures and lockdowns had a detrimental impact on women's employment and women-owned and led businesses. By November 2021, 27% of female-owned and/or led businesses in the Pacific were fully operational compared with 51% of male-owned and/or led businesses (Figure 4; Pacific Trade Invest 2021). More recently established women-owned MSMEs and businesses with more than five employees were more negatively impacted. School closures—coupled with needing to care for sick family members— have reduced the time that women can spend on managing a business or in paid employment.

There is mixed evidence on whether women entrepreneurs in the formal economy or the informal economy have been hardest hit by the pandemic. A survey of 144 women entrepreneurs in PNG found that women with registered businesses experienced more hardship compared to women with unregistered businesses (Center for International Private Enterprise 2021). However, a study in Fiji found female market vendors and farmers tend to have few savings which are not enough to sustain a short-term downturn in income (COVID-19 Response Gender Working Group 2020).

Women entrepreneurs have been using digital technologies to lessen the impacts of the COVID-19 pandemic. In Fiji, a Facebook page created in April 2020 encouraged non-cash trading and bartering of household and work-related items, gaining more than 114,000 (mainly women) members within 2 weeks (Pacific Islands Forum Secretariat 2020). However, in general, women have less access to digital technologies and have fewer digital skills than men (Pacific Women Shaping Pacific Development 2020).

There are some promising examples of COVID-19 support, but evidence is not yet available on their impact. National government stimulus packages for women-owned MSMEs tend to focus on prioritizing credit. These types of loans typically require businesses to be registered, excluding the many women-owned businesses in the informal economy. Some Pacific governments are reaching the informal economy through "one-off" payments, but the amounts are generally too low to meet the needs of informal businesses (Pacific Islands Forum Secretariat. 2020).

DEVELOPMENT PARTNER PROGRAMS AND DATA SETS

Several development partner programs addressing women's economic empowerment in the Pacific are ongoing or have recently closed, although independently published evaluations are not available for all (Table 1).

Figure 4: Status of Pacific Businesses in July 2020 and November 2021

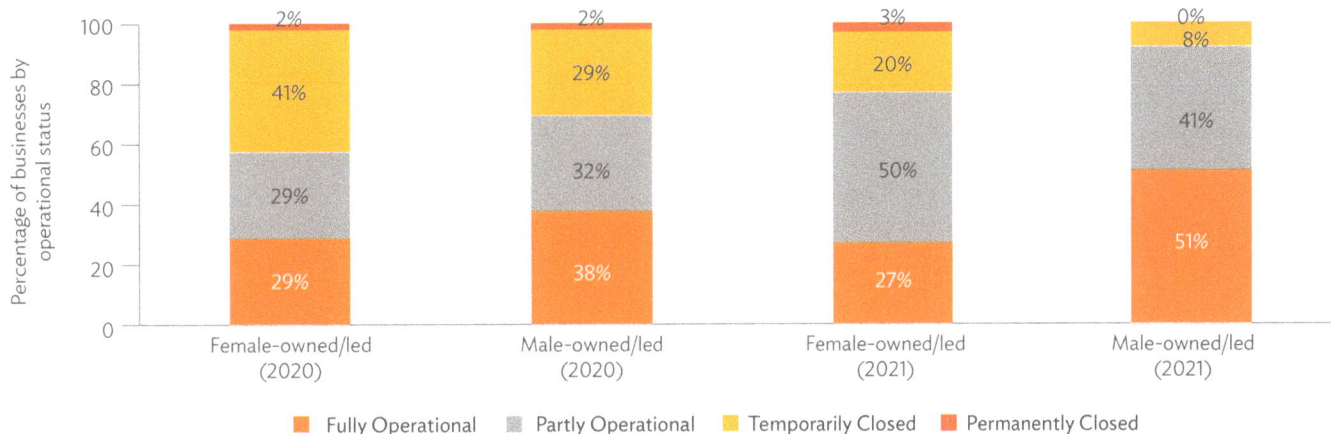

Note: July 2020 results are based on 134 businesses across the Pacific island countries that participated in the regular Pacific Trade Invest Pacific Business Monitor surveys from 29 June to 12 July 2020, with 51% of businesses identifying as female-owned and/or led. November 2021 results are based on eight surveys that took place from January to November 2021. More than 100 businesses participated in each survey, with 43%–53% identifying as female-owned and/or led businesses.

Source: Pacific Trade Invest 2020, 2021.

Table 1: Development Partner Programs

Development Partner Programs	Lessons Learned
• DFAT's Pacific Women Shaping Pacific Development (2012–2021) • DFAT's Market Development Facility (2011–2022) • Pacific Private Sector Development Initiative (2007–present) • DFAT's Pacific Readiness for Investment in Social Enterprise (2016–2021) • DFAT-funded, UN Women and UNDP implemented Markets for Change (2014–2020)	• Strategic partnerships with the government and the private sector can lead to improvements in women's working conditions. • Local groups can positively disrupt harmful social norms. • The "family teams" approach, which encourages male and female family members to work together, can lead to more gender-equitable farming practices.[a] • In financial inclusion initiatives, it is important to engage with male leaders to build support. • Mobile banking services can increase women's independence, privacy, control, and decision-making.

ADB = Asian Development Bank, DFAT = Department of Foreign Affairs and Trade of the Government of Australia, UN = United Nations, UNDP = United Nations Development Programme.

[a] The "family teams" approach uses four workshops: (i) working as a family team for family goals, (ii) planning your family farm as a team, (iii) feeding your family team, and (iv) communicating and decision-making as a family team.

Source: ADB. 2023. *Women's Economic Empowerment in the Pacific Region: A Comprehensive Analysis of Existing Research and Data.* Manila.

Several countries have undertaken economic surveys to global standards, which include sex-disaggregated data in demographic and health surveys, household income and expenditure surveys, multiple indicator cluster surveys, labor force surveys, and World Bank enterprise surveys. There is little information available on how data are informing policy on the economic empowerment of women entrepreneurs and women-owned MSMEs. For example, a study in PNG found that data on women's formal businesses are often "piecemeal and anecdotal, which does not provide reliable data to inform policy (Nagarajan 2021).

RESEARCH GAPS AND RECOMMENDATIONS

Areas for Further Research

- Status and trends of women-owned MSMEs and women entrepreneurs in islands with smaller populations.
- Women's economic empowerment status and trends for women from groups that have historically been marginalized more than others, such as people with disabilities.
- Forms of support to enable women-owned businesses to become more resilient to climate change.
- Effectiveness of COVID-19 government stimulus or support packages aimed at women-owned businesses and women entrepreneurs.
- Incentives for business formalization and the entry points and mechanisms for the expansion of formal businesses.
- Interconnections between women's economic empowerment and VAWG.

POLICY RECOMMENDATIONS

- Repeal legislation that prohibits women from certain types of work.
- Regulators—such as central banks or banking authorities—require sex-disaggregated data to be collected, released publicly, and reported.
- Ratify ILO Convention No. 190 on violence and harassment in the world of work and adopt and enforce sexual harassment legislation and policies in employment.
- Reform tax, finance, and licensing policies and systems to remove barriers and disincentives for women-owned businesses to formalize their businesses.

- Enact parental leave policies that can contribute to changing social norms.
- Introduce childcare policies to help women manage their businesses in the informal economy, or to enable them to return to—or stay at—work after having children.
- Promote and legislate equal remuneration for work of equal value in ways that suit national contexts.

PROGRAM RECOMMENDATIONS

- Encourage financial institutions to accept non-land assets as collateral and increase the uptake of secured transaction frameworks.
- Work with national statistical agencies and designers of international surveys to improve the quality of surveys and include sex-disaggregated questions.
- Develop and implement targeted measures to help self-employed women restart businesses that collapsed or are in "survival mode" because of COVID-19-associated challenges.
- Invest in evidence-based programming that aims to shift harmful social norms that sustain VAWG in the world of work, with a focus on women entrepreneurs and women-owned MSMEs.
- Building on good practice and experience in the Pacific, work with banks to adjust their risk assessment criteria in favor of MSMEs and informal businesses and ensure financial products and services are adapted to women clients.
- Support in-country stakeholders to disrupt social norms that act as barriers to women's businesses, and work with men and boys to support women's economic empowerment.
- Develop the unpaid and paid care provider economy and infrastructure, such as supporting quality and affordable care services.
- Leverage digital access and increase access to mobile phones for women, accompanied by skills building on digital literacy.

Lead author: Chris Hearle (consultant), with guidance from Cindy Bryson (social development specialist, ADB), Ingrid FitzGerald (social development and gender officer, ADB), and Mairi MacRae.

References

Asian Development Bank (ADB). 2019. *Leveraging Trade for Women's Economic Empowerment in the Pacific.* Manila.

ADB. 2023a. *Women's Economic Empowerment in the Pacific Region: A Comprehensive Analysis of Existing Research and Data.* Manila.

ADB. 2023b. *Women's Economic Empowerment in the Pacific Region – Summary.* Manila.

Center for International Private Enterprise. 2021. *COVID-19's Impact on Women-Owned and -Operated MSMEs in Papua New Guinea.* Port Moresby.

COVID-19 Response Gender Working Group. 2020. *Gendered Impacts of COVID on Women in Fiji. Fiji Women's Rights Movement.* Suva.

Fiji Women's Crisis Centre. 2013. *Somebody's Life, Everybody's Business! National Research on Women's Health and Life Experiences in Fiji (2010/2011): A survey exploring the prevalence, incidence and attitudes to intimate partner violence in Fiji.* Suva.

Food and Agriculture Organization. 2019. **Country Gender** *Assessment of Agriculture and the Rural Sector in Samoa.* Rome.

Government of Fiji, Bureau of Statistics. 2016. *Employment and Unemployment Survey 2015–2016.* Suva.

International Finance Corporation (IFC). 2019a. *Tackling Childcare: The Business Case for Employer-Supported Childcare in Fiji.*

IFC. 2019b. *Waka Mere: Commitment to Action.*

International Labour Organization (ILO). 2017. *Improving Labor Market Outcomes in the Pacific: Policy Challenges and Priorities.* Suva.

ILO. 2020. *Pacific labour market review 2020.* Suva.

S. Lawless. et al. 2021. Gender equality is diluted in commitments made to small-scale fisheries. *World Development.* 140 (2021).

V. Nagarajan. 2021. *Women and Women's Business Access to Finance Market Research in Papua New Guinea.* Sydney.

Pacific Islands Forum Secretariat. 2020. *Information Paper No. 4: Economic Empowerment of Women.* Suva.

Pacific Trade Invest (PTI). 2020. *Pacific Business Monitor: Impact on Female-Owned/Led Businesses.*

PTI. 2021. *PTI Pacific Business Monitor 2021 - Female-Led Focus.*

Pacific Women Shaping Pacific Development. 2020. *Thematic Brief: Gender and COVID-19 in the Pacific: Emerging Impacts and Recommendations for Response.*

Pacific Women. 2021. *Final Report 2012–2021.* Sydney.

United Nations Economic and Social Commission for Asia and the Pacific. 2020. *Micro, Small and Medium-sized Enterprises' Access to Finance in Samoa: COVID-19 Supplementary Report and Recommendations.* Bangkok.

World Bank 2021. Women, Business and the Law. Washington, D.C.

Finding Balance 2023: Benchmarking performance and building climate resilience in Pacific state-owned enterprises

In March 2023, the Asian Development Bank Pacific Private Sector Development Initiative launched *Finding Balance 2023: Benchmarking Performance and Building Climate Resilience in Pacific State-Owned Enterprises*. The publication reviews the financial performance of state-owned enterprises (SOEs) in nine Pacific Island economies, identifies the risks that state-owned power utilities are facing as a result of climate change, and assesses policy mechanisms available to governments and SOEs to improve their resiliency and sustainability.[1] The period covered includes the first year of the coronavirus disease (COVID-19) and its associated border closures and lockdowns.

The study is the seventh in the *Finding Balance* series, which tracks the progress and impact of SOE commercialization in participating countries. This principle of commercialization—which allows SOEs to operate under similar legal and governance parameters to private companies—underpins SOE reform efforts throughout the Pacific and is compatible with broader government goals of inclusive economic growth. In addition to the survey of SOE financial performance, this edition of the *Finding Balance* series has a special focus on the profound risks posed by climate change, and how governments and their state-owned utilities are acting to mitigate its effects and build resiliency. The study shows how efforts to commercialize SOEs and partner with the private sector are assisting SOEs to respond to climate change.

STATE-OWNED ENTERPRISE PORTFOLIO PERFORMANCE 2015–2020

The SOE portfolios of the nine economies covered by this study are dominated by infrastructure service providers (e.g., airports, seaports, power, water, sanitation, broadcasting, postal services, and telecommunications), and include a range of other commercially oriented undertakings such as transport and banking (Figure 5).

The study shows that while average SOE returns have improved during 2010–2020, they still fall short of covering their costs of capital. Only two of the nine SOE portfolios produced a return sufficient to cover capital costs during 2015–2020. Three produced average returns on assets (ROAs) and/or average returns on equity (ROEs) below zero over this period (Table 2).

In most countries, these low returns are achieved despite subsidized capital, monopoly market power, and ongoing government cash transfers. The low returns on SOE investment dampen economic growth. Despite sizable investments by governments in the SOEs—representing up to an estimated 37% of total fixed capital in each country—they contributed only 0%–15% to gross domestic product (GDP) in 2020 (Figure 6).

Figure 5: Composition of State-Owned Enterprise Portfolios, FY2020

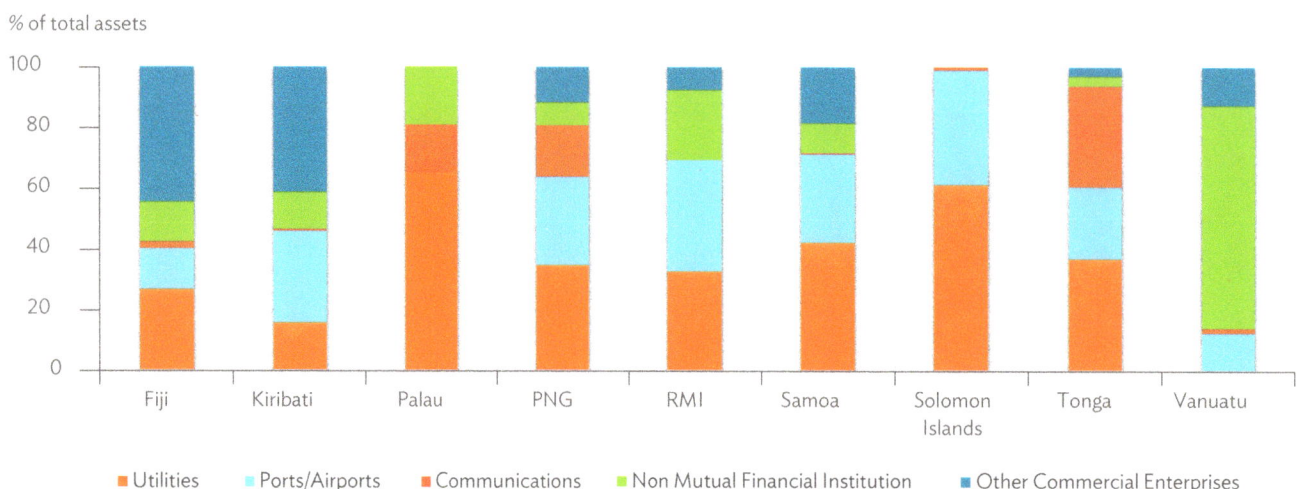

FY = fiscal year, PNG = Papua New Guinea, RMI = Republic of the Marshall Islands.

Note: In all charts and tables in this policy brief, fiscal years end on 30 June for Samoa and Tonga; 31 July for Fiji; 30 September for the Marshall Islands and Palau; and 31 December elsewhere.

Source: ADB. 2023. *Finding Balance 2023: Benchmarking Performance and Building Climate Resilience in Pacific State-Owned Enterprises*. Manila.

Table 2: State-Owned Enterprise Portfolio Performance Indicators

Country	Average Return on Assets FY2015–FY2020 %	Average Return on Equity FY2015–FY2020 %	Contribution to GDP 2020 %	Total Portfolio Assets 2020 $ million
Fiji	3.4	7.4	2.6	2,002
Kiribati	2.4	2.9	14.6	172
Marshall Islands	4.6	7.0	8.8	198
Palau	(1.2)	(2.7)	5.4	198
Papua New Guinea	(0.2)	(0.1)	1.2	2,866
Samoa	0.4	0.8	4.1	694
Solomon Islands	7.1	9.8	4.1	386
Tonga	2.7	4.8	5.8	304
Vanuatu	(2.2)	(21.4)	(0.1)	312

( ) = negative, FY = fiscal year, GDP = gross domestic product.

Source: ADB. 2023. *Finding Balance 2023: Benchmarking Performance and Building Climate Resilience in Pacific State-Owned Enterprises.* Manila.

Figure 6: State-Owned Enterprise Contribution to Gross Domestic Product versus Total Fixed Capital Controlled by State-Owned Enterprises, FY2020

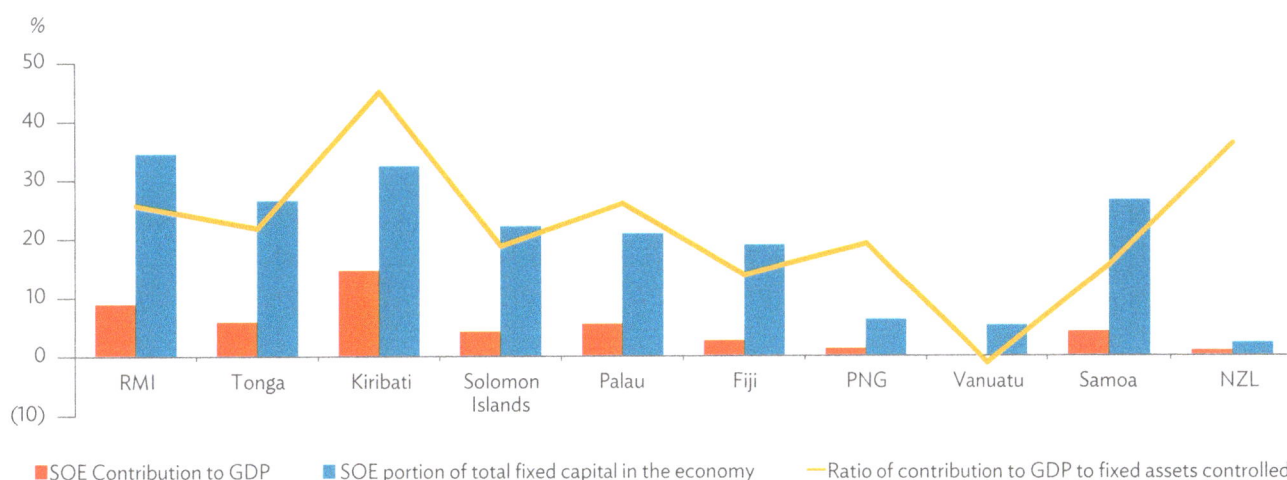

- SOE Contribution to GDP
- SOE portion of total fixed capital in the economy
- Ratio of contribution to GDP to fixed assets controlled

FY = fiscal year, GDP = gross domestic product, NZL = New Zealand, PNG = Papua New Guinea, RMI = Republic of the Marshall Islands, SOE = state-owned enterprise.

ADB. 2023. Finding Balance 2023: Benchmarking Performance and Building Climate Resilience in Pacific State-Owned Enterprises. Manila.

SOEs benefit from ongoing government equity contributions. These are typically provided to finance assets and working capital, retire debt, and absorb accumulated losses to allow SOEs to function. SOE net profits exceeded the value of government transfers in only four countries during 2015–2020.[2] The majority of countries with cumulative net losses during 2015–2020 required ongoing government contributions. For countries in which ongoing government contributions were required, these were equivalent to 0.02%–3.74% of GDP (Figure 7).

Across the Pacific region, GDP contracted by 6.2% in 2020 and 1.4% in 2021, largely due to travel restrictions, which cut off a substantial portion of tourism inflows, labor mobility, and trade.[3] This economic contraction was mirrored in the SOE portfolios of each country, with five of the nine countries recording lower returns in 2020 than in 2019 (Figure 8). In contrast, the Marshall Islands, Kiribati, and Palau saw improved portfolio performance because of a range of factors, including sharply reduced expenses in the power utilities sector in Palau and the Marshall Islands (with revenue remaining steady), an increase in community service obligation payments to Air Kiribati, and a surge in non-core revenue in the Kiribati Plant and Vehicle Unit.

Figure 7: Average Government Transfers to State-Owned Enterprises, FY2015–FY2020

% of average GDP

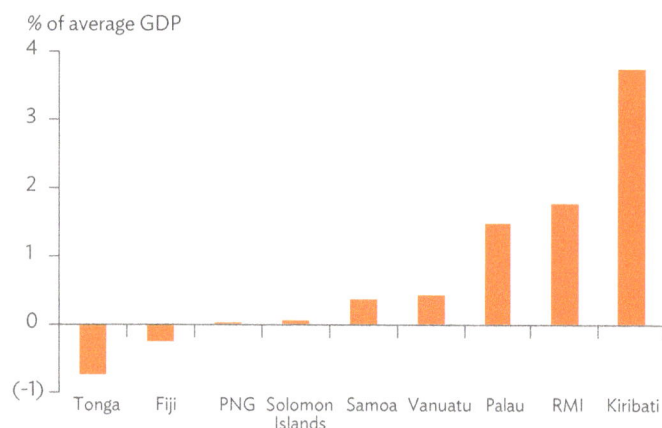

( ) = negative, FY = fiscal year, GDP = gross domestic product, PNG = Papua New Guinea, RMI = Republic of the Marshall Islands.

Source: ADB. 2023. *Finding Balance 2023: Benchmarking Performance and Building Climate Resilience in Pacific State-Owned Enterprises.* Manila.

Figure 8: Average State-Owned Enterprise Return on Assets by Sector in Survey Countries, FY2015–FY2020

%

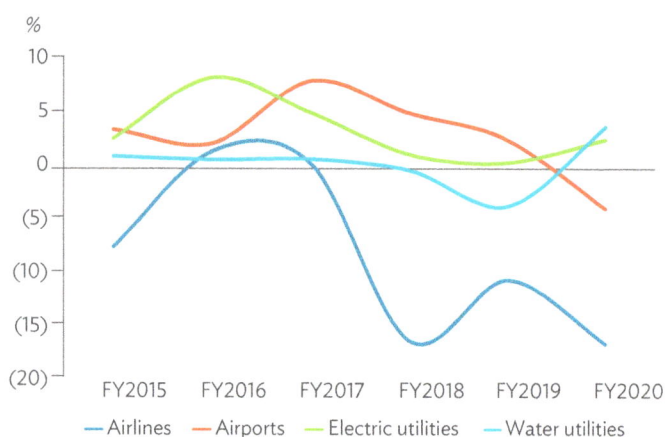

— Airlines — Airports — Electric utilities — Water utilities

( ) = negative, FY = fiscal year.

Note: Electric utilities include the Public Utilities Board (Kiribati), and the Palau Public Utilities Corporation, which also provide water services. These have been excluded from the water utilities group.

Source: ADB. 2023. *Finding Balance 2023: Benchmarking Performance and Building Climate Resilience in Pacific State-Owned Enterprises.* Manila.

SOEs involved in air travel and tourism—most notably airlines and airports—were the hardest hit by border closures. Revenues were down by an average of 34% for airlines and 27% for airports in 2020 compared to 2019, which weakened portfolio returns in five of the seven countries with SOE airlines and all five countries with airport SOEs.[4] Five of the seven airlines in the SOE portfolios were financially vulnerable before 2020, with some generating losses in each of the 5 preceding years; COVID-19 only exacerbated the need for restructuring. Power and water utilities, in contrast, did not face a substantial reduction in revenues or profitability, despite shouldering some of the costs of government responses to COVID-19. For power utilities—most of which are large consumers of diesel fuel—the drop in fuel prices was a major driver of reduced operating costs. For water utilities, demand remained strong in 2020 and the utilities covered by the study saw improvements in profitability.

LIMITATIONS OF THE SOE MODEL

The poor performance of SOEs in the Pacific is consistent with what is commonly observed in other regions of the world, illustrating a fundamental flaw in the SOE model. Government ownership provides incentives for political accommodation at the expense of commercial outcomes, and political pressures to overstaff and undermaintain. Many governments view SOEs not as commercial ventures but as political liabilities. SOEs are managed to reduce political risks, not optimize commercial returns and operational efficiency. Politicians have difficulty taking commercial decisions that have political costs. Governments rarely allow necessary restructuring measures or price increases for SOE outputs when elections are pending.

Because of these inherent challenges to state ownership, the SOE model was never designed as a long-term ownership model, but as a vehicle to transition from state to private provision of services. However, governments are typically reluctant to pursue privatization, often due to concerns about near-term political costs. Instead, the focus has been on creating legal, governance, and monitoring frameworks to mimic the conditions and incentives that private sector firms face. Pacific countries continue to make important progress in this regard, but these frameworks do not in themselves guarantee improved SOE performance. What is crucial is the political will to require SOEs to realize positive rates of return and hold them accountable for results. When this will exists, a robust SOE legal framework facilitates commercial outcomes.

CHANGING HOW THE STATE SUPPLIES GOODS AND SERVICES

An alternative to continued government ownership is privatization, which international experience demonstrates results in more efficient service provision.[5] Privatization is the most effective means of locking in efficiency gains created by restructuring government departments into SOEs and ensuring further improvements in operational performance. Private ownership brings much-needed commercial discipline, capital, and expertise, and can also open new markets. When privatization transactions failed, they were usually poorly prepared or lacked regulatory frameworks to ensure that public monopolies did not become private monopolies.

Privatization's economy-wide effects on government budget, growth, employment, and investment have also been shown to be positive. A study involving 18 countries with significant privatization programs reported substantial budget inflows from privatization, accounting for nearly 2% of annual GDP.[6]

Partnerships with the private sector—through full or partial privatization, supported by robust regulatory arrangements—are the most effective mechanisms for long-term improvement in state asset productivity. Where full privatization is neither politically feasible nor the most suitable reform mechanism, partial privatization (public listings, joint ventures, and public–private partnerships [PPPs]) can help to improve SOE performance.

STATE-OWNED ENTERPRISE REFORM HIGHLIGHTS, 2015–2022

All nine countries participating in the study adopted some measures to commercialize their SOEs and/or introduce greater private sector participation during 2015–2022. Highlights include:

- **Fiji:** privatizing 59% of Fiji Ports Corporation Limited in 2016 and 24% of Energy Fiji Limited (EFL) in 2019, with a further divestment of 20% in 2021, and it is intended that 5% of EFL shares will be listed on the South Pacific Stock Exchange and given to existing customers; EFL signing a power purchase agreement for the development of a 5 megawatt grid-connected solar plant in 2021; and enacting a new Public Enterprise Act in 2019, which improved the governance and commercial framework for SOEs.

- **Kiribati:** completing a competitive tender for a PPP to rehabilitate the Betio Shipyard in 2017, placing the Captain Cook Hotel under a management contract, and building capacity in the SOE monitoring unit to implement the SOE Act.

- **Marshall Islands:** adopting a comprehensive SOE Act in 2015 and operationalizing an SOE monitoring unit in the Ministry of Finance in 2018.

- **Palau:** completing a competitive tender for a 16 megawatt solar generation PPP in 2020; issuing Executive Order 465 in 2021 reaffirming Palau's National Policy for SOE Governance and supporting SOE commercialization; preparing an SOE bill to implement the policy; undertaking a series of corporate planning and governance reforms in the Palau Public Utilities Corporation in 2021, consistent with the SOE Policy; establishing an independent regulatory process for setting cost recovery electricity and water tariffs for the Palau Public Utilities Corporation; and adopting a new Public–Private Partnership Policy in 2021.

- **Papua New Guinea:** adopting a new SOE Ownership and Reform Policy in 2020 and subsequent amendments to the Kumul Consolidated Holdings Act in 2021 to strengthen governance and transparency; operationalizing the PPP Act through the adoption of amendments and regulations in 2022; completing a competitive tender for a container terminal concession for the ports of Lae and Port Moresby in 2017; signing two independent power producer (IPP) contracts for gas-fired power generation in 2019; and launching a competitive tender for a solar IPP in 2021.

- **Samoa:** amending the SOE Act in 2015 to establish a new SOE ministry under a minister of SOEs; privatizing Agricultural Stores Corporation in 2016; and contracting four IPPs to add 10,000 kilowatts of solar generation capacity.

- **Solomon Islands:** signing the power purchase agreement and reaching financial close for the Tina River Hydro Public–Private Partnership Project; corporatizing airport operations into the Solomon Islands Airport Corporation; issuing a new SOE Ownership Policy in 2018 to guide future investments, link the target capital structure and dividend of each SOE to its business plan, and strengthen the coherence of SOE oversight; and Cabinet endorsement of amendments to the SOE Act to strengthen the director selection process and promote the participation of women on SOE boards.

- **Tonga:** completing a competitive international tender for a 6 megawatt solar IPP, which reached financial close in 2020; completing a concession agreement for Tonga Forest Products Ltd assets and plantation on Eua Island; amending the SOE Act in 2020 and 2021 to strengthen governance and monitoring provisions; completing a competitive tender for an integrated cargo handling concession at the Queen Salote International Wharf; and cabinet endorsement of skills-based SOE director selection guidelines in 2020.

- **Vanuatu:** preparing a new SOE bill in 2018 based on the 2013 SOE ownership policy, which calls for the commercialization of SOEs and the establishment of a centralized ownership and monitoring function within the Ministry of Finance and Economic Management; and the further privatization of National Bank of Vanuatu in 2020, with the Ministry of Finance reducing its ownership share to 44%.

CLIMATE CHANGE AND STATE-OWNED ELECTRIC UTILITIES

As governments in the Pacific work to improve the financial sustainability of their SOEs, they must incorporate strategies to address emerging risks, including climate change, which is rapidly becoming existential. Climate scientists expect equatorial regions will confront more intense and more frequent disasters, such as cyclones, floods, and coastal inundation as global temperatures increase in the coming decades. While Pacific countries contribute very little to global greenhouse gas emissions, they are setting ambitious emissions reduction goals, investing in adaptation, and making plans for the worst impacts of climate change.

State-owned utilities are important players in these efforts. In eight of the nine countries in this survey, state-owned utilities were the dominant providers of electricity, 78% of which on average in 2020 was generated from thermal fuel, resulting in high electricity tariffs (Figure 9), price volatility, and potential insecurity of supply.

Pacific state-owned utilities that are more commercialized may be more inclined to respond to commercial incentives to decarbonize or to reduce the financial risks associated with climate change. These SOEs may also be more inclined to invest in protecting their assets from climate-induced physical damage, given its impact on financial sustainability. However, to optimize these choices, SOEs must operate in a policy environment conducive to commercialization.

Figure 9: Average Price of Electricity in Pacific Countries Compared to World, 2014–2019

US cents per kilowatt hour

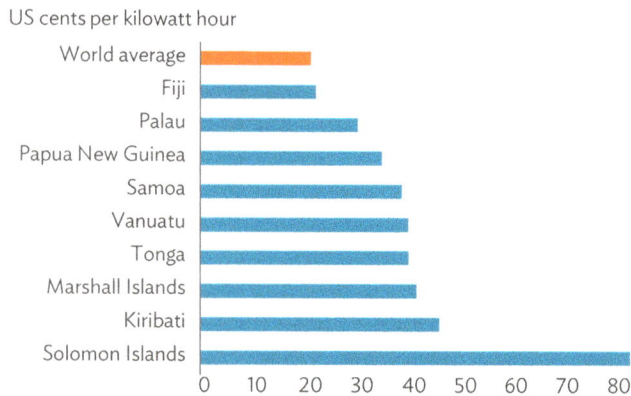

US = United States.

Source: World Bank Group. 2020. *Doing Business Report* (DB16-20 Methodology). Washington, DC.

Beyond establishing robust governance frameworks within which their SOEs can operate commercially, governments have several policy tools with which to assist their SOEs to adapt to climate risks and build resilience. These include: (i) introducing climate-related financial risk disclosures and supporting SOEs to make such disclosures, as is required under the Papua New Guinea Climate Change (Management) Act 2015; (ii) raising capital to finance public investment in climate resilience and decarbonization, in particular through development partners, green bonds, and specialized funds; and (iii) supporting private investment in renewable energy generation, including in existing state-owned electric utilities.

Lead authors: Laure Darcy, state-owned enterprise reform expert, Pacific Private Sector Development Initiative; Chris Russell, state-owned enterprise reform expert, Pacific Private Sector Development Initiative; and Arjuna Dibley, Head of Sustainable Finance Hub, University of Melbourne.

Endnotes

[1] Fiji, Kiribati, the Marshall Islands, Palau, Papua New Guinea, Samoa, Solomon Islands, Tonga, and Vanuatu. ADB. 2023. *Finding Balance 2023: Benchmarking Performance and Building Climate Resilience in Pacific State-Owned Enterprises.* Manila.

[2] Fiji, the Marshall Islands, Solomon Islands, and Tonga.

[3] Asian Development Outlook database (accessed 19 June 2023).

[4] Core revenue for Airports Kiribati Authority (AKA) grew by 8% from 2019 and 2020; it was the only airport in the surveyed countries were core revenue increased in 2020. Source: AKA draft 2020 financial statements.

[5] Many international studies have shown that SOEs perform less well than private sector companies. For example, a 2004 study by the Norwegian Institute of International Affairs concluded "using return on assets as the measure of performance and carefully controlling for market structure and a range of factors that may have an impact on company performance; we find that the performance of SOEs is indeed inferior to that of private companies." Three surveys by the Organisation for Economic Co-operation and Development (OECD) and the World Bank contain similar findings.

[6] N. Birdsall and J. Nellis. 2003. *Winners and Losers: Assessing the Impact of Privatization.* World Development Vol. 31, No. 10, pp. 1617–1633.

Addressing the paradox of forestry imports amid abundant local resources

Forestry products have historically been the leading export commodity for Solomon Islands, accounting for an estimated 60% of total export value in 2022. Despite its significant contribution to the economy in terms of revenue and employment, the sector has been plagued by unsustainable logging practices, leading to deforestation and environmental degradation.

IMPACT OF COVID-19

In addition to rapidly shrinking forest resources, the forestry sector faced challenges due to reduced global trade in forestry products and supply chain disruptions caused by restrictions related to the coronavirus disease (COVID-19) pandemic. In 2022, logging output contracted by 22%, marking the fourth consecutive year of decline. Exports of logs and timber fell by 20%, resulting in a 33% decrease in export duties from logging (ADB 2022).

Solomon Islands traditionally relies on an export-led economy, with goods and services exports constituting more than 40% of the pre-COVID GDP (2010–2019). However, the decline in exports of this major commodity hampered the country's ability to pay for imports necessary to meet domestic demand, particularly due to the limited domestic manufacturing industry.

STRONGIM BISNIS IN SOLOMON ISLANDS

Strongim Bisnis (Strengthen Business) is an Australian Government initiative in Solomon Islands contributing to Australia's economic partnership objectives including private sector resilience, improved livelihoods, and inclusive growth. The program collaborates with the private and public sectors to identify market opportunities and co-invests with businesses to test new products, services, or business models across the country.

ADDRESSING THE PARADOX

Amid a decline in international demand for forest products, domestic market opportunities became more appealing for the private sector across various industries. Paradoxically, although forestry products are the largest export commodity, the country still imports value-added wood products such as furniture, flooring, plywood, and even wooden pallets due to limited local value-addition.

Strongim Bisnis partnered with Kolombangara Forest Products Ltd (KFPL)—a major exporter of Solomon Islands products—to invest in a commercial pallet plant. The goal was to meet the needs of local exporters and logistics providers, create job opportunities, and reduce reliance on imported value-added wood products. Historically focused on exporting rough plantation wood to high-value markets, KFPL ventured into value addition to meet domestic demand. Even before the plant was fully operational, SolTuna became KFPL's first customer, placing a minimum order of 5,000 pallets annually.

OPERATIONAL SUCCESS AND ECONOMIC IMPACT

The plant is fully operational, employing six highly trained full-time workers. It utilizes local plantation timber to produce high-quality pallets made from Forest Stewardship Council certified timber, emphasizing environmental and social sustainability. Within the first 6 months of 2023, KFPL produced and sold 4,500 pallets, saving the economy at least SI$1.04 million on imports. The company is exploring new markets for this recently launched product among other exporters and logistics providers in Solomon Islands.

> "It is amazing that the Solomon Islands exports so much timber, but we have to import it back as finished products. Now, we are processing and adding value to our own plantation logs, employing local people, and adding value to the economy."
> *KFPL General Manager Edwin Schramm*

DIVERSIFICATION THROUGH DOMESTIC MARKET FOCUS

Another example of *Strongim Bisnis* support is for Tropic Group Builders—a local construction company that invested in cabinetry and furniture making—which started in January 2021. They have made significant progress in the local furniture market, supplying major buyers such as Solomon Water, Solomon Power, SolTuna, and Bank South Pacific. This resulted in a 10% growth in both the value and volume of orders in the first 6 months of 2023.

In addition to the timber sector, the private sector in other industries also made investments to meet domestic demand in collaboration with *Strongim Bisnis*. Solomon Airlines—the national carrier—launched its first-ever domestic tourism campaign when the country's borders were closed to international tourists. Even after the border reopening, the airline continues the campaign, recognizing the potential value that the domestic market offers. Another example is Island's Own, a local enterprise that launched its range of toiletries using locally produced coconut oil, leading a major importer in the country to halt the import of similar products. Furthermore, in 2022 *Strongim Bisnis* partnered with Kokonut Pacific Solomon Islands, the country's largest exporter of coconut oil, to produce cocoa for the domestic market.

INCREASING RESILIENCE THROUGH DOMESTIC MARKET FOCUS

Although the size of domestic markets for niche products is small, investing in commercially viable products and services for the local market can have a cumulative impact on increasing the overall resilience of the economy. This argument becomes even stronger in the context of declining forestry product exports due to increasing deforestation. The success of *Strongim Bisnis* initiatives indicates that a heightened focus on domestic markets—resulting from the COVID-19 situation—can bolster the resilience and diversification of the Solomon Islands economy, aligning with the vision of the Government of Solomon Islands.

Lead author: Jawad Khan, Business Partnerships Director – Technical Sectors, Strongim Bisnis

Photos: Eugene Kerekere

References

Asian Development Bank. 2022. *Pacific Economic Monitor: The Future of Social Protection in the Pacific.* Manila.

International Trade Centre. *Trade Map* (accessed 15 June 2023).

A.Riddle. 2023. *COVID-19 and the U.S. Timber Industry (Report No. R46636)*. Congressional Research Service.

Minister for Education and Human Resource Development and Member for Gizo-Kolombangara Hon. Lanelle Tanangada and the Australian High Commissioner Rod Hilton observing the Kolombangara Forest Products Ltd. pallet plant in action

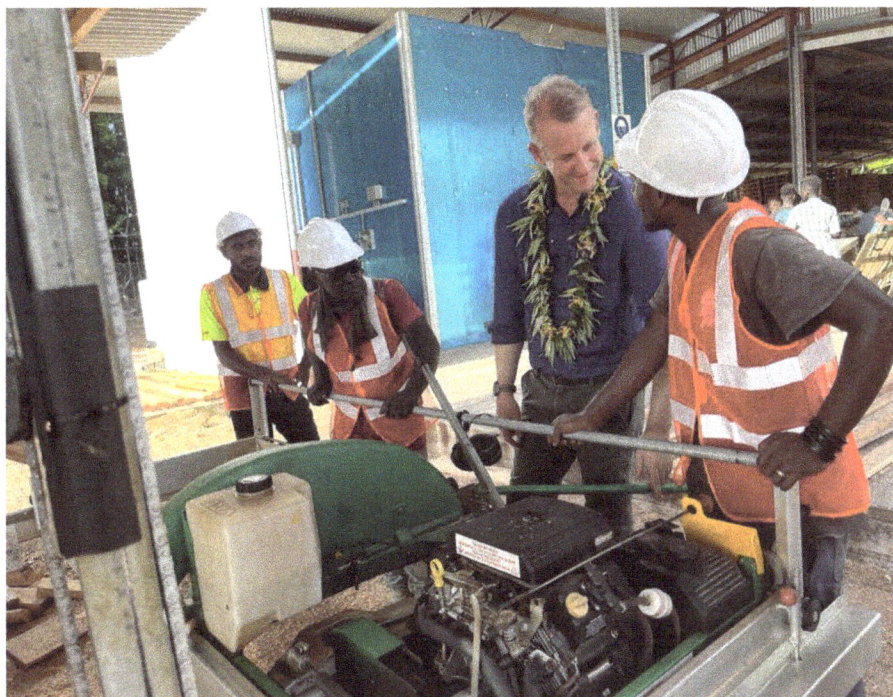

Australian High Commissioner Rod Hilton discussing the new pallet plant with Kolombangara Forest Products Ltd. staff.

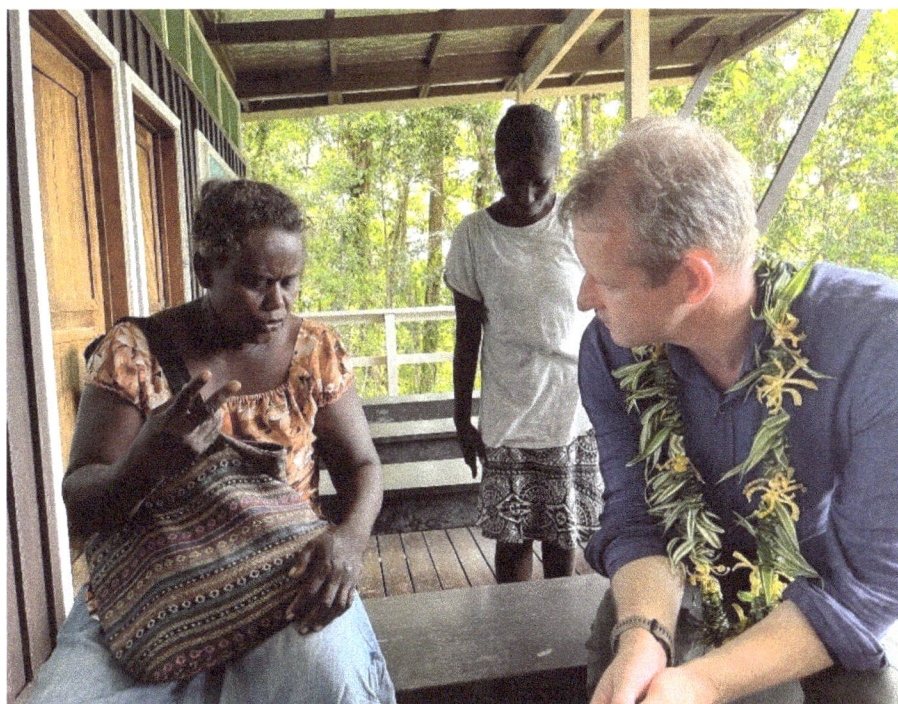

Kolombangara community member Mebilyne Fred speaks to Australian High Commissioner Rod Hilton about the Australian-funded out-grower training she completed and plantation challenges faced by growers.

Minister for Education and Human Resource Development and Member for Gizo-Kolombangara Hon. Lanelle Tanangada addresses guests at the community launch.

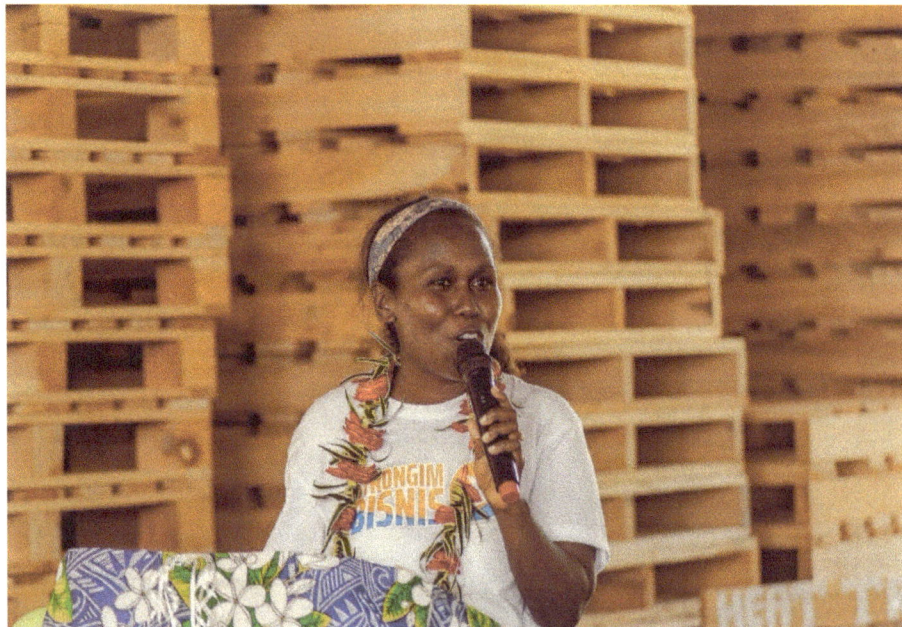

Strongim Bisnis Business Advisor to the Timber sector Zefi Keritina speaks at the community launch.

Kolombangara Forest Products Ltd. pallet plant staff demonstrate the construction of pallets from logs through to the finished product.

Nonfuel Merchandise Exports from Australia
(A$; y-o-y % change, 3-month m.a.)

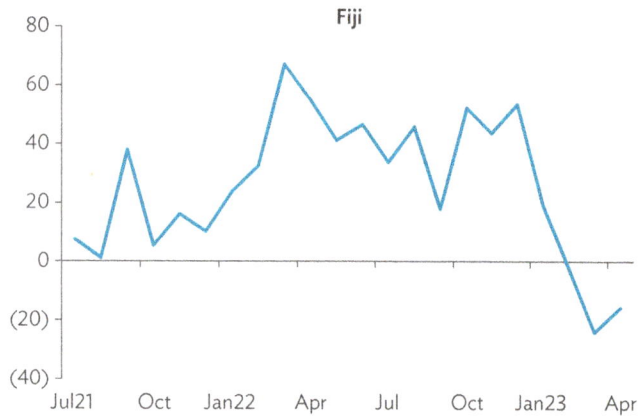

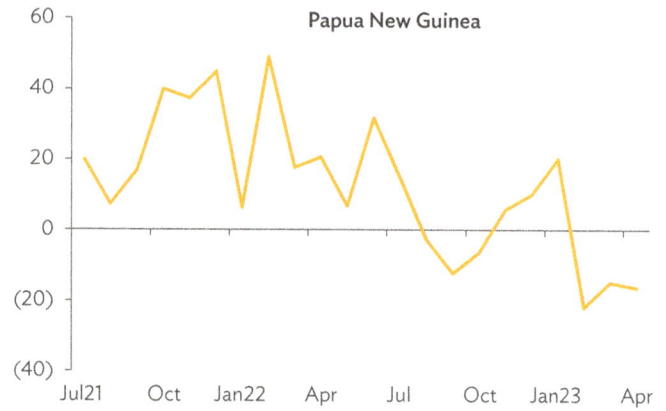

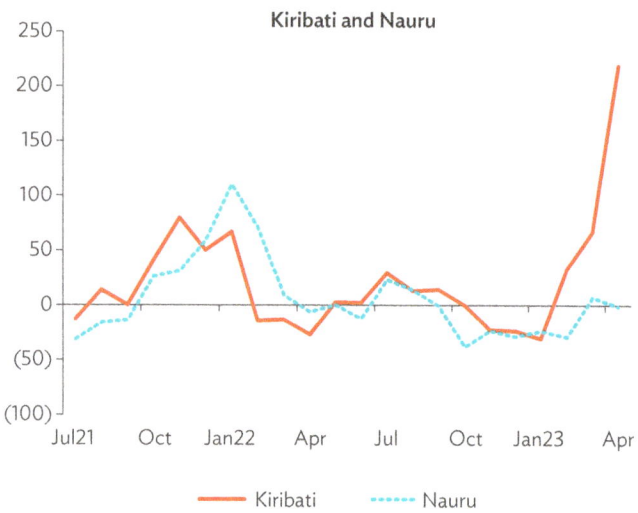

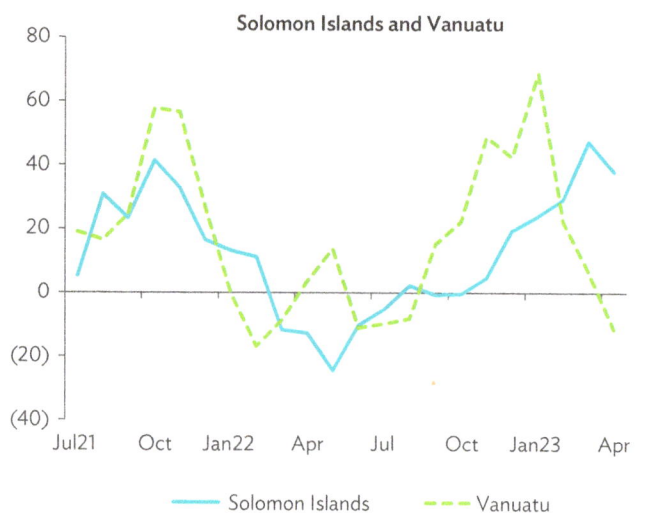

Fiji

Papua New Guinea

Kiribati and Nauru

—— Kiribati   ····· Nauru

Solomon Islands and Vanuatu

—— Solomon Islands   - - - Vanuatu

( ) = negative, A$ = Australian dollar, m.a. = moving average, y-o-y = year-on-year.
Source: Australian Bureau of Statistics.

Nonfuel Merchandise Exports from New Zealand and the United States
(y-o-y % change, 3-month m.a.)

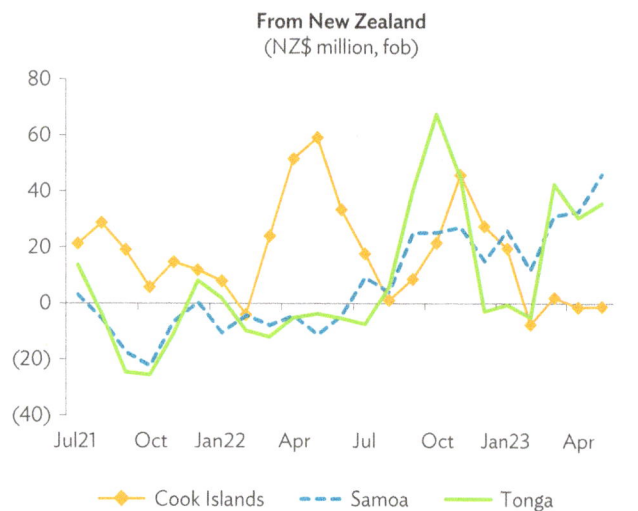

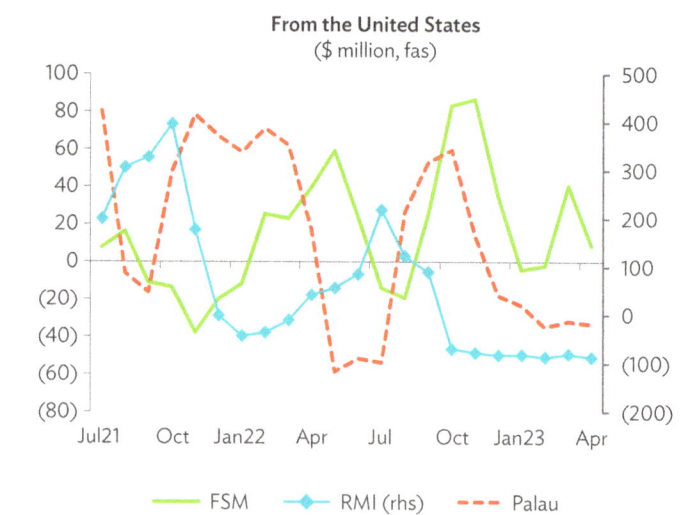

From New Zealand
(NZ$ million, fob)

◆—— Cook Islands   - - - Samoa   —— Tonga

From the United States
($ million, fas)

—— FSM   ◆—— RMI (rhs)   - - - Palau

( ) = negative, fas = free alongside, fob = free on board, FSM = Federated States of Micronesia, m.a. = moving average, NZ$ = New Zealand dollar, rhs = right-hand scale, RMI = Republic of the Marshall Islands, y-o-y = year on year.
Sources: Statistics New Zealand and United States Census Bureau.

Diesel Exports from Singapore
(y-o-y % change, 3-month m.a.)

Fiji

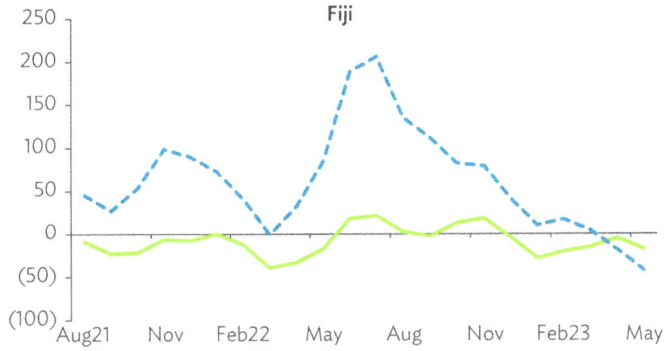

Papua New Guinea

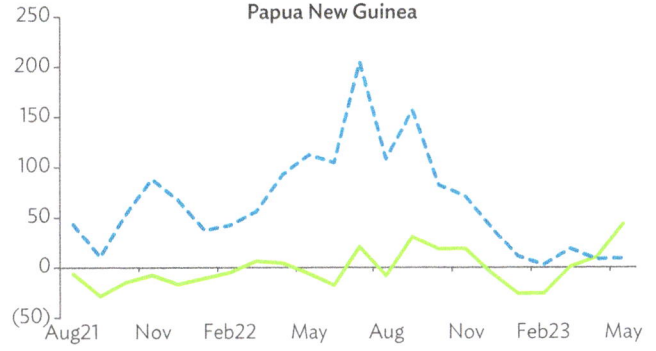

Samoa

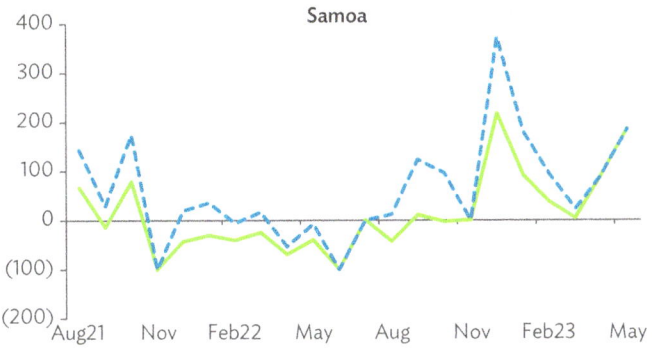

Solomon Islands

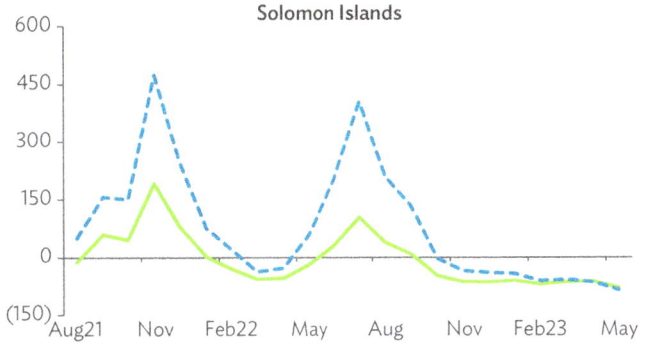

— Volumes   - - - Values

( ) = negative, m.a. = moving average, y-o-y = year on year.
Source: International Enterprise Singapore.

Gasoline Exports from Singapore
(y-o-y % change, 3-month m.a.)

Fiji

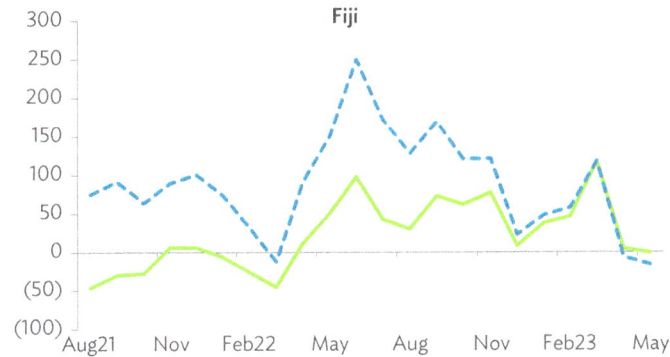

Papua New Guinea

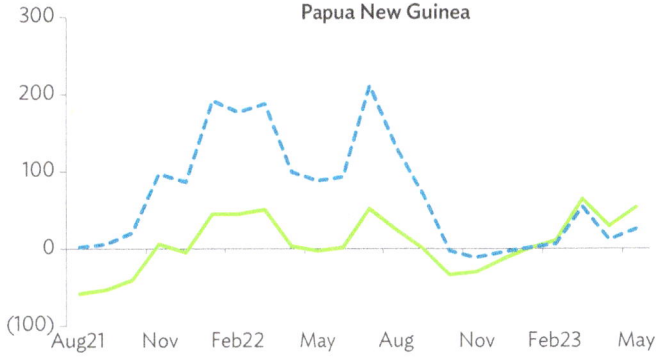

Samoa

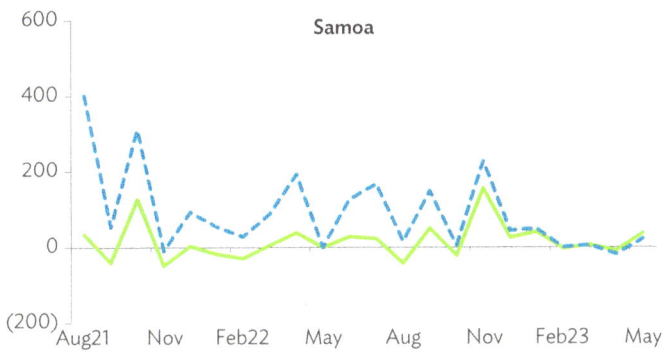

Solomon Islands

— Volumes   - - - Values

( ) = negative, m.a. = moving average, y-o-y = year on year.
Source: International Enterprise Singapore.

Departures from Australia to the Pacific
(monthly)

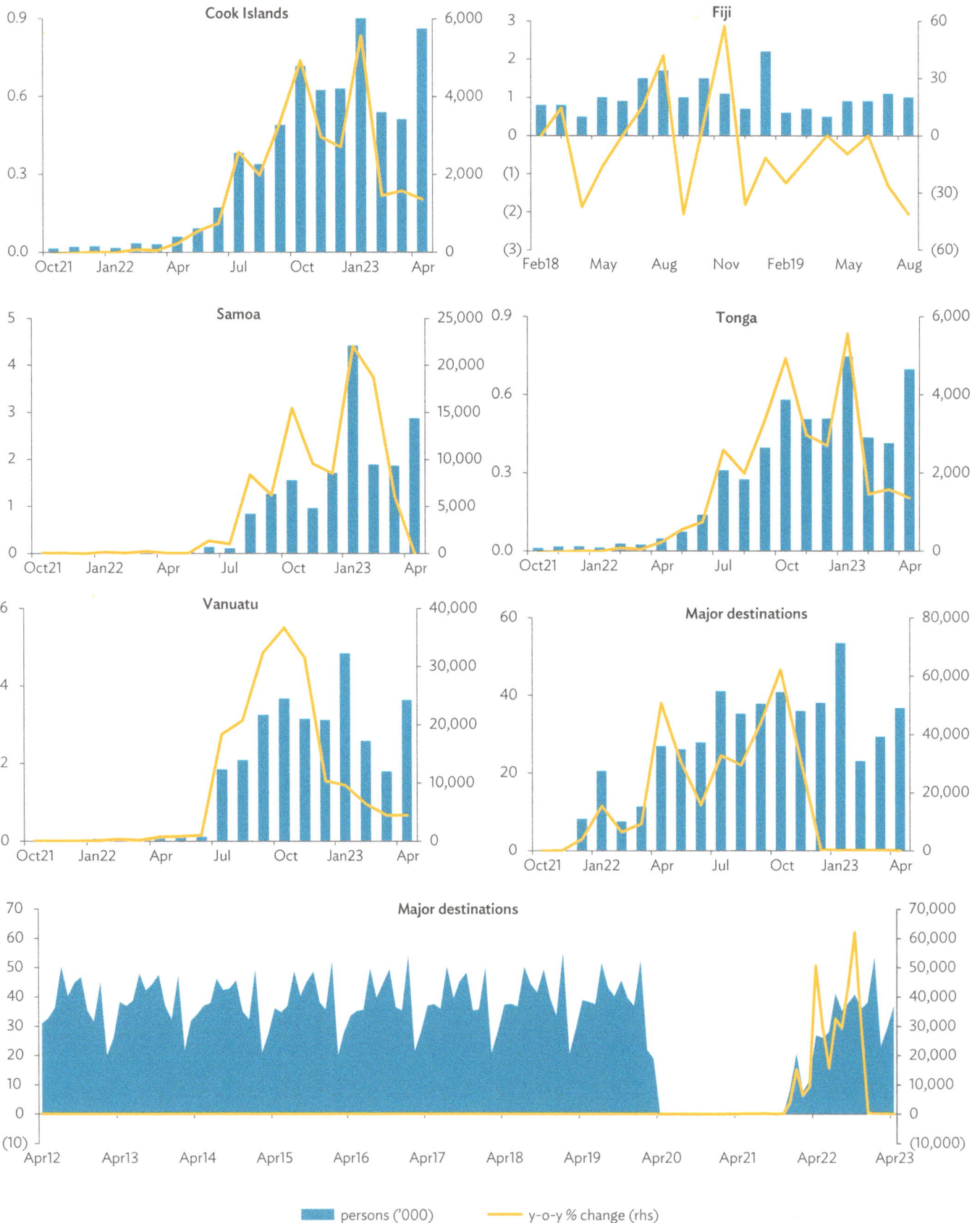

Cook Islands

Fiji

Samoa

Tonga

Vanuatu

Major destinations

Major destinations

persons ('000)   y-o-y % change (rhs)

( ) = negative, rhs = right-hand scale, y-o-y = year on year.

Source: Australian Bureau of Statistics.